8 Princi
Further Education:
Progressing Your Career
to an Elite Level

ISBN: 978-1-7393992-0-7

This book is dedicated to my wife, Sarah, and son, Stanley.
I love you both dearly. You're the best.

Table of Contents

Chapter 1

Introduction

You want a pay rise, you want a promotion, you want a career that you can be proud of, but think that your time has come and gone? Think again. Your time has not come and gone, far from it. You have probably just followed a common trait of not focusing on your own education within a chosen field that could offer all the things that you want. I should know, this was me. I was guilty of this but found a way to counter a common perception that people cannot outperform themselves if they do not achieve early in their career. If you are like I was or simply want to progress your career, then read on and learn how you can achieve more than you ever dreamt of.

My journey from a street sweeper to a PhD. University lecturer in 11 years has led me to author this book. I will detail the 4 foundational principles and 4 elite principles that led me to my success as I want you know that you can do the same. My journey did not start with success at all, it started from a position of anger and embarrassment following a work related disciplinary. I was twenty-six years old and wanted to progress a career but had no idea how and with no guidance available to help me. This book offers the guidance that I wish I would have had, and that you are lucky enough to have. Follow the 8 principles and you can achieve more than you ever thought was possible. Honestly, if I can do it, you can too.

In November 2010, I stood in an urban street in South-West England in minus five-degree weather with a sweeping brush in hand and a map detailing my daily street cleansing duties. My thoughts were certainly not focused on the working day ahead of me or the star jumps that I had to do in order to warm up, rather on a disciplinary decision that I thought had been an injustice. The result of this disciplinary decision meant that I had to sweep streets by myself for twelve months, a distinct temporary demotion from the street cleansing driving position that I had occupied. My wages had decreased, my confidence was damaged, and I was a laughingstock amongst my colleagues. More importantly, however, I had a wife and a two-year-old son at home to support. I must at this point make it clear to you that I recognise street sweeping as a significantly important job in our society and is incredibly challenging. It was just not the job that I wanted when I gained a street cleansing driving position.

I was at this point in my life not educated past average GCSE results and a failed attempt at entry level accountancy qualifications, and had spent my late teens living in Germany working in a factory. Although fun, my time in Germany had not progressed any occupational plans of any kind, which left me without any specific work skills or completed apprenticeship as some of my friends had. As you can imagine, this did not lead to many future job prospects and placed me far behind my friends when it came to nice cars, designer clothes, and attending events. That said, my focus really was not on these things. I did however want to provide greater things for my family and improve our standard of living. My work situation at this point was not delivering this.

Twelve months is a long time to ponder this dilemma, especially when you are working alone and doing a job that you consider as punishment. Not surprisingly, my initial thoughts were anger and embarrassment. These, however, did not last as long as expected. They couldn't really as it was becoming increasingly difficult to sleep and was affecting my home life. So come this extremely cold day in November 2010, my thoughts had changed to avenging my perceived injustice by achieving greater accolades than that held by the person I believed was responsible for me sweeping the streets alone in the cold weather. Although this felt like progress and made each day a challenge rather than a nightmare, I had zero clue of how I could achieve my new vision. In short, this sort of achievement does not happen to uneducated people like me, does it?

I found myself in a difficult position as I had no-one to guide me on what I wanted to do. In fact, I did not even want to discuss the idea with anyone with fear that I would be laughed at and called delusional or unrealistic. Well, maybe they would be right. Maybe I was unrealistic, and my future was to complete the twelve months disciplinary period, take my punishment, and return to a street cleansing driving position. But they could be wrong. Could I achieve greater than was expected of me. The one thing I was sure of was that it would not be easy, and I had to commit fully to the goal.

What was not so clear was actually what the goal would become. The idea to be more successful than the person I held responsible for my downfall was energising, but it really was not measurable. I mean, how would I ever know if I had achieved as I had never previously looked up to higher positions within a company. I was unlikely to be promoted to any position within the organisation that had pleasingly demoted me, was I? I was equally unlikely to want to work with the individual that had energised my new thoughts by punishing me, was I? Questions that I had no clue how to answer, or even whether they needed answering. Again, there was no guidance available to me, which caused me to find my own path.

On reflection, I don't think that I ever answered the questions. This may have been because I was overcome with a fresh motivation which occupied my focus, or just that I began to think of what my first step would be towards my goal. Either way, my mindset had significantly shifted towards positivity, and moved away from the anger and embarrassment that had started my process. In all honesty, this did take some time but happened naturally. Thinking back, I cannot remember the exact point in time that it happened. What I did know, however, was that I had a goal and that my destiny, whatever that was going to be, was up to me. Nobody else, just me.

This book tells the story of what happened next. Eleven years of intense study, promotion, business start-up, and of course many failures. The result of this dedication has been far beyond what I could have ever dreamed of. I now use Dr. before my name, have multiple letters after my name, am a senior professional, a lecturer at university, and have a lovely house. Please do not think that I am bragging at all; none of this would have been possible for me without education, which I started once I developed my purpose as a result of my twelve-month punishment period. Believe me, if you follow the 8 principles that I share with you, you have the potential to achieve these things too. I am not saying it is easy. I am saying that it is possible.

Further education has truly changed my life and made me who I am today. Don't waste any more of your time wishing that your fortunes will change for the better, start the first foundation principle today, and begin the journey to improving your life for yourself. Your pathway will of course be different from mine. But a pathway is there for you to find. Don't be the one wishing for a pay rise or promotion; be the one that actively makes it happen.

Honestly, if I can do it, then you can too.

Chapter 2
Principle 1 - Find a Purpose

The first section of this book sets out the 4 foundation principles. These are based on the experiences that I had that took me from a punished street sweeper to supervisor, and then onto interim operations manager. This progression was more than I, or anyone around me, ever thought could have been possible. I am testament that it is achievable for you also to reach this level, and of course, levels above. Let's start with the foundation principles to build your base.

The wants

Wanting something will inevitably give you a purpose to have it. That said, not everyone will want the same thing. Some will want designer clothes, some will want fancy cars, some will want a house extension; all very different things. In one environment, however, there is a want that I have identified being requested by nearly everyone. The environment is a work performance meeting, and the want is more money. I certainly do not criticise that everyone wants more money; money is a necessity. I do, however, think that your own actions have more chance of increasing your salary than simply asking your employer to increase your salary. Which is actually in my experience almost impossible to achieve in this way.

When I write that nearly everyone asks for more money, I really mean it and have vast experience for making this claim. I understand that more money per hour/day/week/month will improve your standard of life as you will be able to afford more of the things that you want, and that prices are rising which increases the cost of everyday items. My journey also contains this want in various forms. I am no different, I want more money too. I just learned to think of it in another way; a way that is available to you by developing yourself and, therefore, adding value to others and the organisation that you represent.

I remember very clearly being a street sweeper and feeling lucky enough to meet with my manager to discuss my performance. In hindsight, I think I overthought the importance of this meeting as it occupied my mind for days leading up to it. I had mentally practiced the various approaches in which I could ask for more money, ranking the ideas on which would achieve the biggest pay rise. Of course, as I came to learn all too well, none of my approaches would be successful. This is because often, a pay rise is not even in the picture. Rather, a performance meeting 'ticks boxes' and literally sometimes only adds another piece of paper to your personnel file. I tried, nonetheless. The answer was normally what could only be described as a laugh.

This is, however, not confined to frontline workers. As I have come to learn, the request for more money does not cease when you achieve supervisor and management levels. In fact, the request is sometimes even emailed in preparation of the performance meeting. There appears to be a race to reach the highest salary possible within any full-time job as if that is the achievement. Yes, it may be an achievement, but is it sustainable? This is especially in question if your skillset has not advanced enough to meet your required outputs. Unfortunately, this has resulted in many significant company positions being filled with incompetent people, leading teams to underperform. Which ironically does not enhance their chances of a pay rise. Rather, this can lead to failing teams that produce undesired outcomes which can result in reduced profits for the organisation.

I remember this was evident when I held a performance meeting with a supervisor. We both had very different thoughts on his performance. He thought he was delivering perfectly, whereas I was aware of numerous complaints about his performance, conduct, and overall lack of compliance. Although I knew that the 'money' question was going to come at some point, I did not anticipate how and when it would be presented to me.

I barely had time to shake the supervisor's hand before he stated, "I am worth more money, I want more money, and I get more money." Well, to say that this was not the best opening gambit is a vast understatement, especially considering that my role in that meeting was to have this individual motivated at the close of the meeting. In all honesty, I would rather have seen this employee leave the company than have a pay rise, but saying this would not motivate him in any way, would it? Of course not. So, I asked a question that I like to ask in such a situation: what are you going to do to achieve a pay rise? To which I received a very common response, a blank stare with no answer.

This is sadly also a common response in such meetings with performing employees. It must be understood that every organisation will have a limit regarding how much they can pay employees, otherwise they would not make a profit, which is why most organisations exist. This may seem unfair, but that is not something that you can change at this point no matter how much you plead. I held a performance review with a supervisor who was worth every penny of their current salary based on their performance but would need to gain further qualifications and experience to meet the grade for a salary enhancement. I made this clear and offered guidance on how it can be achieved. It is very rare, but this employee reacted positively to this information and actively pursued self-development. I personally found this to be a very positive outcome of the meeting. Better than giving 50 pence more per hour that was unsustainable under company policy, I offered a means by which a career could progress: education. It is worth noting at this point that this employee did progress their education and has since been promoted numerous times, enhancing their salary significantly. Any coincidence? I think not.

This is an interesting point as up to the writing of this book; no employee has ever asked me what education could progress them within their respective company or specific role in a performance meeting. Everyone seems to want the financial improvement immediately, and without offering the company anything extra. Based on my experience, extensive progression, and subsequent success, I can tell you that you can achieve your wants if you focus on your own development. Even if you don't get that 'quick' pay rise that you think may be warranted to you.

Change of mindset

As mentioned in the introduction of this book, my initial thoughts following my perceived punishment were anger and embarrassment. This not only took a lot of energy from me, but it also did not let my mind rest. My thoughts were on this every working minute and every moment that I was not working. I can only imagine how hard it must have been to be with me during this time; not much fun would be an understatement. I am sure that these were testing times for my family and friends.

The extremely cold November day in 2010 was the point that I told myself that my mindset had to change. I could not go on like this, so miserable and cold. Agreed, I could not change the weather, but it was in my gift to change my mindset. But I had no real idea how to do it. However, luckily for me, there was no timescale required for my mindset alteration. My wife, Sarah, did not put any pressure on me at all. When in all honestly, she could have felt fully aggrieved by the situation that I had landed us in and expected me to 'turn things around' quickly, maybe even by getting a better paid job. The one comment that I remember from Sarah most vividly was, "I love you no matter what job you do." At a time when I felt like I had failed, this gave me strength in the situation. I was extremely lucky to have this support.

On reflection, I think I subconsciously set a timescale for myself. I was acutely aware that any positive thoughts were very new to me as they had only been negative ones for some time. For this reason, I somehow knew that I needed to react quickly before I possibly reverted to thoughts of anger and embarrassment. The action I took was to focus my mind on these new ideas every minute and hour that I swept the streets. My daily working duties became my platform for creativity and personal thinking, allowing time to develop my plan. I enjoyed my work now. Which was something that I had not believed could be possible during my 'punishment of 12 months', as each working day before this was quite frankly dreadful. To explain, my job during this period was to work as a 'dilly person'. This involved working completely alone with a cleansing trolley and a selection of cleansing tools. To add to this, I was not allocated shelter during my breaks which meant I had to find a café or betting shop in which to sit and eat my lunch. It was difficult for sure, but now I was developing my plan.

I realised early on in my plan developments that there were no rules or barriers, no one to make fun of my ideas, and no limit to what I could achieve. All these things were possible as I was on my own all day working. Even if was working in a team, I would not have shared my ideas with my colleagues. I had a solid belief that they would not have been supportive of me. Whether this assumption was right or wrong, I could not risk the possibility of derailing my plans by feeling anger and embarrassment again because of something that someone had potentially said about me. Another reason for not saying anything was that I had no idea what I was talking about as my development had not really even begun yet.

What had begun was my desire to be in a higher position than the person that I felt had punished me. This was a thought that was constant throughout this stage of my development. But quite frankly, I was very aware how ridiculous this idea sounded, I mean, I was merely a street sweeper, and he was a contract manager. Worlds apart. This was simply unachievable even in my wildest dreams. But, for some unknown reason, I did not stop thinking about it. Something that I am very thankful for and is a true example that you too should dream big, and sometimes bigger than you think is even possible.

Wanting to be in a higher position than this individual would first need me to understand what position he was in. This from the outset seemed very clear, he operated as a contract manager. But that in the grand scheme of things did not explain his purpose within the workplace. To understand this, I had to observe him, which was possible only twice daily; once at the beginning of the shift when I 'signed in', and again at the end of the shift when I 'signed out'. A very familiar format to many manual working jobs, I am sure.

I found out quickly from my observations that his sole driver appeared to be power. This would be evident in many different forms, but his requirement for control was constant. The finest example I can give was his allotted parking space. The parking on site was not necessarily at a premium, there was always space especially when he arrived at site early. However, irrelevant of space or time, he would use this space. You may read this and think that a manager should possibly have a personal parking space and in certain circumstances I would agree. The main problem with this specific example is that he had to break the site safety rules by walking across a 'no walking permitted' section of the site to get to the office in which he worked. In essence, this parking space should never have been permitted, rather condemned as off-limits. I remember the day that this was openly challenged to him by an employee to which his response summed his attitude up perfectly, "I am the Manager and will do what I want." I am assuming, but I think that you may also know a manager with similar traits.

What I could not work out during these observations was how or why this person held the role of contract manager, a role that appeared to be a very senior role within the business. Yes, he had the power that he needed for himself to function, but how did he achieve it? This was the actual question that I knew I had to answer if I wanted to be in a position such as his, or to achieve my desired goal, a position higher than his.

Although I was unable to answer this question at this point in my development, I felt comfortable as I knew that I no longer had a negative mindset. My mindset was now positive, in that I had a distinctive and positive goal that I was focusing on daily. I made a bold statement to myself at this time that I would become a better manager than him. Or, whatever better meant anyway.

Material things

Let's not forget the need to have material things. These also offer great purpose for wanting to progress in a career. This was certainly no different for me. These material things are in no doubt different from person to person and hold varying attractions, and at financial values that can be at times poles apart. For instance, successful professional football players will probably not be satisfied with a scoring bonus that affords them an extra pair of football boots. Their wants are likely to be much higher and remain so based on their expectations.

My situation, as a street sweeper, provided a very modest income. Therefore, I was not accustomed to expensive treats. This, however, didn't mean that material things were not on my radar, quite the opposite in fact. As a football and rugby fan I wanted the usual, tickets and shirts. I just could not afford them and lived by the value taught to me by my dad. I remember vividly being told as a 14-year-old, "if you can't afford it, you can't have it." One of the values that I have lived by ever since I did not get the pool table that I wanted. Well, I never had enough money to buy it anyway.

I held true to this value throughout my twelve-month punishment period. This was extremely challenging as I was earning less money than I had been used to due to my wages dropping for the full twelve months, so I could not afford as much. Therefore, I had to save for longer to get material things. Which was no more frustrating than a guitar that I had set my sights on. This desire may have been easier to dismiss had I not been forced to see it. I must explain. This guitar took prime spot in a music shop window display that was on my daily street cleansing route. Twice daily, I had to walk past this window with the guitar staring at me. I wanted this guitar with every fibre of my being, I just could not afford it. So, I could not have it.

Of similar nature was a painting that I saw once whilst out shopping with my wife. This painting was particularly appealing to me because it was by Bob Dylan, a musical icon of mine. My first thoughts when viewing this painting were, when did Bob Dylan start painting? And how much does it cost? This painting was well and truly outside of my price range, but it did not deter me from going into the shop to look closer. I am convinced that by questioning the shop assistant, there was a clear understanding between us both that I did not have the required funds to purchase this painting. Very correct. And so, I walked away disappointed. By this time in my development, my wife was aware of my focused career mindset and subsequently offered that I could get the painting if I earned a specific salary. A very kind gesture considering that Bob Dylan is not my wife's favourite artist for music, painting, or anything else.

It could have been very easy for me to view these two material things, the guitar, and the painting, both of which I could not have, as failures as I could not afford them. This was not the case at all. My mind was clearly focused on progression, and if progression resulted in that I could have these things once I have succeeded, well, that will do just fine. These two material things formed a part of my purpose to develop my education and move towards a financial position that would allow me to afford such things. I found this to be very positive and to this day, I continue to have material things that I want but cannot yet have. I am sure that I won't achieve some of them, however, they never fail to provide me with a purpose.

There are, of course, certain circumstances where you just cannot wait to make a purchase, no matter how much you would rather not. I found this out when we had a TV indoor aerial that was completely unpredictable. One moment it will work and the next it could stop, returning to function whenever it felt like it. I tried to wait until it completely failed before buying a new one. I held strong until I was watching a very important football match and missed a ten-minute period of play when all the vital moments in the match happened. That was it. I needed to get a new one now. This became a short-term purpose and one that I achieved very quickly.

It was apparent to me that purposes came in many different guises. In this time, I came across yet another form, wanting to recreate an experience or adventure that held valuable memories. Again, aligning with my value of can't afford, can't have, my wife and I saved for two years after our marriage in order to go away on our honeymoon. We had chosen Egypt as our destination and were both extremely excited about the trip. We were right to be. It was wonderful. This included the airport as we had booked the 'lounge'. This allowed us as much food and drink as we wanted. All, without the chaos that an airport can present as it was a quiet room. It was just us two in this restaurant for around two hours. It was a perfect start and the luxury continued in Egypt at a level that I had never experienced before. I wanted it again. So much so that I spent the final three days of the week trip planning in my head how we could be able to do it again. Honestly. There I was at poolside with a notepad detailing a saving plan for accumulating enough money to return. This was now an additional purpose that only added focus to my development.

The question you are probably asking yourself at this stage of this book is, so how do I start accumulating the money required to get my material things? Well, your focus at this stage should be in setting a foundation for understanding your personal financial position. Once known, this too will become a purpose for progression as a better financial position will allow for more of your material things. If you do not know your financial position, how will you be able to measure whether you have improved?

The first action to take is to become aware of your income versus your expenditure, keep receipts, and tally up at the end of the week or month, depending on your work pay frequency. For those of you who are familiar with accounting may consider this approach rather simple. I agree, this is a simple approach, but at this stage you are building the foundation principles. Principles that will lead to career progression, which in turn will lead to more of the material things that you may desire. Documenting your finances only takes time and effort, not money, ironically.

Therefore, this development is free to all.

Looking back, I think that the material things that I did not have gave me far more motivation than those that I was fortunate enough to buy. I did however save enough money to buy the guitar, but am yet to purchase the Bob Dylan painting. Not because I have not reached the salary challenge set to me by my wife, rather because I want to do more to earn it as it is an expensive purchase. I personally prefer to have the motivation than the painting at this present time. This still motivates me today.

Foundation Principe 1 – Find A Purpose

The Wants – *You can achieve your wants if you focus on your own development. Far more effective than asking for that 'quick' pay rise or promotion.*

Change of Mindset – *There are no rules or barriers, and certainly no limits to what you can achieve. You must dream big, have distinctive goals, and remain positive whatever the results. Make a bold statement to yourself that you can achieve it.*

Material Things – *Material things hold varying attraction from person to person. Don't discount the motivation that wanting something material gives you and use it as energy.*

Chapter 3
Principle 2 - Locate the Ladder

Job titles

I did not have any idea where I stood on the company's ladder, or in fact that a ladder exists at all. I knew my job title, Street Cleansing Operative, and quite honestly had no interest in anybody else's role in the company before my mindset change. Once my mindset changed, it was very different. I was working alone all day and had ample time to think about these things. I was now looking at the bigger picture, which resulted in me learning about my surroundings, my colleagues, and the people ranked above me in the organisation. There was no need me looking below my position in the organisation as my role was considered the bottom rank. I must reiterate that I do not see the role of a street sweeper inferior in any way. Having worked the role, I know exactly how difficult it is and what it offers each community.

When looking up, the first thing I noticed was many roles above me had the same, or very similar, titles. We had for instance three 'contract managers' within our depot, all of which appeared to carry out different duties. This did not make understanding their job any easier for me, but it did get me thinking. Is this a title that they give themselves? Is this just a title used in our depot? And, most importantly for me with my new focus, can I achieve the role of contract manager?

In addition to these questions, I also wanted to know where all of these 'contract managers' came from. To try and answer this, I had to speak to my colleagues, ensuring that I masked the questions that I asked them, so they did not think that I had plans to reach such a position. There was, however, one colleague that I could talk to no matter how unrealistic my ideas were, my father. He had been at this point working as a refuse collector/refuse driver, within the same depot as the street cleansing division, for over twenty-five years, and informed me that two of the contract managers had actually started their careers as front-line workers. One started as a refuse driver and the other as a street cleansing operative. Really, this one individual progressed to contract manager from my exact position, a street cleansing operative. This was positive news as it signified that I could possibly also make the leap into management at some point in my career. If they could do it, why could I not?

The only other position within the company that I was aware of at this point was that of Managing Director. This was only because we had all received a letter in the post from the Managing Director, although everyone knew it was a blanket message, telling us all how successful the company was. I don't know about my colleagues but in my position, I did not care about the company success at all. In my eyes, I had failed and that was all that bothered me. I remember also being offended by the opening to the letter, "Dear Colleagues". Colleagues? I thought well, *why you haven't been to see us*. And if a street cleansing operative was off sick for a day and it would be noticed by the community, would the same impact be felt if the managing director was off? I did not think so.

Irrelevant of this thought, or any others for that matter, what was important was my attendance at work. I had to ensure that I worked every day with no absence or sickness as my pay was reduced by the punishment, and so every penny counted. This, and the fact that I was on a final written warning, meant that I had to be fully compliant with whatever the contract managers requested of me. I began to feel that all of the three contract managers were acting against me. This, however, may have only been my perception of the situation as I had no idea what these 'senior people' were saying to each other about me behind closed doors. Or, in fact, whether I was worthy of their interest at all, negative or otherwise.

One thing I was certain of was how powerful the phrase "I am the Contract Manager" was. It was irrelevant what the situation was, if the phrase was used the conversation stopped immediately and the employee complied with the demand, whatever the demand was. It appeared that no-one would challenge the contract manager position, and that contract managers had privilege above the front-line employees. This was cemented in my thoughts on a dark December morning in 2010. I was going through a period of fitness training and started to run or cycle into work, leaving my house at 05:15 am to ensure that I had time for my heartrate to return to resting before my shift started. When I arrived on this particular morning, I was met by a contract manager at the door stating that "Contract Managers don't need to run as they have a better standard of life". As I was the same as my colleagues, this comment was not to be challenged, rather to be accepted. I did accept it without responding but did think that this individual probably felt that he needed to try and humiliate me as he could not have run or cycled the distance that I did. Whether I was right or not, it made me feel better in myself and smile when I thought back on it throughout the day on my street sweeping route.

As my goal was to be at, or above, this position of management, I made a promise to myself. A promise that I would make every effort to never use my job title as power to win a discussion. In my eyes, all people are equal, and I have come to learn that we just have different reporting responsibilities. Therefore, each person's ideas need to be reviewed on merit, not on their job title. I truly believe this still today.

My most interesting finding surrounding job titles also came at this point in time. Although the contract managers appeared untouchable and supremely powerful due to their job titles, they did change behaviour. This behaviour change came when the regional manager arrived on the scene, a new role within the company that I was not familiar with. This was a person that us street cleansing operatives only began to see during a period of failure, or when a pay rise was in debate. When the regional manager arrived, the contract managers would strive to show a professional manner when talking with their teams. Words seemed to be pronounced correctly, slang or swear words were avoided, and the phrase "I am a Contract Manager…" was not used. Some of my colleagues took advantage of this situation. I do not blame them at all. I would not like to count the number of annual leave and new uniform requests that were submitted when the regional manager was in attendance. Needless to say, all requests were accepted, and with a smile on the contract managers face. A false smile, but a smile, nonetheless.

Your place in the company

I forget who, but somebody had made me aware of something called an organisational chart or organogram. Initially I had no idea what this was but knew that I needed to find out quickly. As I came to know, this document visually shows the employees, and respective roles, of an organisation, or a specific section of an organisation, if it has many different layers and departments. Once I understood this it was vital to me that I viewed the street cleansing organisational chart as maybe it would help my development.

This was, however, not so simple. The organisational chart was not openly displayed on the wall in our depot, and I did not really want to risk the humiliating consequences of asking a contract manager if I could see it, as I thought that I would have been laughed at. I had no choice. I had to ask a contract manager. The response was not what I expected. I was immediately taken into the back office and presented with a file, which contained the organisational chart. I thought this was very helpful from the contract manager, but of course he had to win somehow. This came in the form of a comment that I remember very clearly still today. As soon as I focused my eyes on the organisational chart, the contract manager pointed to his name and said, "that is where I am, a manager". There appeared to be no limit to his desire for power.

What I remember from my brief look at the chart was that my name was not on it, neither that of any of my colleagues. We were represented as street cleansing operatives. Whereas the managers were represented by their actual names. Although I realised that the chart would have needed to be extremely large to contain all of the 100+ street cleansing operatives, it did not make me feel valued, rather, it made me feel quite worthless. I could, however, not show this emotion to the contract manager as it would have indicated a weakness. I simply thanked him for the help and departed the office. He never even asked me why I wanted to see it.

As this happened before my shift began, I had the rest of the working day to reflect on what I had seen. My thoughts initially focused on how unprofessional the documents seemed. There was no company logo and was not up to date as it contained a contract manager that had left the company some months before. As my computer skills and knowledge were not advanced at this stage, I could not determine how the document was created, but I assumed that it was not of a high standard due to the inconsistencies in font size and type. The other clear inconsistency was that at the very top of the chart was a photo of the managing director. To me, this said that the only person worthy of a photo was the person at the very top.

Towards the end of the day, my thoughts had changed to what this document meant for my development. Now I knew that a route to the top is possible, at least in theory anyway. The progression route was set for me, Supervisor, Contract Manager, Regional Manager, Managing Director. I knew that I had potentially over-simplified the journey, but it aligned my direction, and I was happy with that and knew that I would need to take one step at a time. So, my focus was now on becoming a street cleansing supervisor. The first step was to observe what they did, and therefore, what I would need to do in order to achieve this goal.

The 'perks'

The first observation that I made was how the supervisors and contract managers were treated by the front-line employees. It was interesting to me that I started to notice things that I would have normally overlooked. I started also to see some of my colleagues in a different light as at times their actions appeared deliberate to gain advantage over other employees. The most apparent and deliberate attempts were made in order to gain additional overtime. The majority of the overtime was worked on weekends and many employees would start their efforts first thing on a Monday morning for the following weekend.

What was immediately clear was the amount of tea and coffee that was bought for the contract managers and supervisors. It was astonishing. The measure of the managers power could have been measured by how many drinks they had bought for them. I remember some of my colleagues came to work equipped with money bags full of twenty pence coins to serve this purpose, as a cup of tea or coffee costed this exact amount. They presumably did not want to be in a position that they could not take advantage of a situation by not having the money to buy the hot drinks.

This was so prominent within our depot that I remember on multiple occasions seeing three or four cups of tea lined up for a contract manager. I thought at the time that some of the drinks would be cold by the time that they got around to consuming them. They may have even been thrown away. But, never, and I mean never, was an offer of a drink refused by a contract manager or supervisor

The buying of drinks was not only a gesture without prompt, but it was also often suggested, albeit mostly in a humorous manner. An example of this coming one Friday with the possibility of potential weekend overtime being raised with a contract manager. This was met with what became a common phrase, "I would like to, but my throat is a bit dry". Which everyone knew that a cup of tea or coffee was required. It was no secret that these transactions took place and was actually not a behaviour that changed even when the regional manager visited. It was clearly accepted. Interestingly, no one ever complained about the situation. I guess that both parties were gaining something. The managers and supervisors' copious volumes of caffeine and the front-line workers overtime, or other perceived benefits.

I needed to also focus my observations, however, more specifically on what was my first desired promotion, the role of the street cleansing supervisor. I chose to observe two specific supervisors as they were new to our depot and, therefore, I had no prior preconceptions about their behaviour. However, I was certainly no expert in observing human behaviour. I did not write down the observations or plan in advance. I just wanted to know if the street cleansing supervisor role is one that I could do, or even if it was one that I wanted.

My first observation was a positive one. The supervisors were actually very friendly, which appeared to lead to the front-line employees wanting to work for them. This was contrary to what I had come to expect from the contract managers, as their approach seemed to be 'you must do' rather than what I was seeing from the supervisors' 'please can you do' attitude. The impression I received was that the front-line workforce would rather be guided by a supervisor, but in the greater picture, had no choice but to answer to the contract manager.

Very different from my structured day as a street cleansing operative cleansing a scheduled route, a supervisor was able to move about freely. A 'perk' that appealed to me greatly at the time as I did not have any choice surrounding my daily duties. A supervisor would arrive on my route at different times, on different days, and to no clearly identified frequency. These on route visits from a supervisor actually became something that I looked forward to as there was never an altercation or confrontation. The visits did require some form of paperwork completion each time regarding cleansing or personal presentation standard, however, once this formality was complete, we would talk about non-work-related subjects for a short while. I thought very highly of the supervisors and wanted to achieve high street cleansing standards for them.

It was through the non-work-related discussions with the supervisors that I was able to begin to plot my direction towards becoming a street cleansing Supervisor myself. I had found out at this point that the only reason that one of the supervisors got the job was by demonstrating qualifications, or in his own words, "I had an education". This made me believe that it was an education, or qualifications, that set this individual apart from the crowd. I had to believe what he said and go by his version of events as I had nothing else to use as guidance.

This was the first discussion I ever had regarding education leading to a benefitting a career. In hindsight, I should have asked the most important questions at the time, *what education? What qualifications?* I did not ask. I felt far below this supervisor in stature within the company and did not want him to ask why I wanted to know, or even worse, communicate my questioning to my colleagues or the contract managers.

At least this gave me a starting point for my development based on something that I believed to be true. An education could advance my career. My quest was now to confirm that it was the right thing to do.

Education works

The timing for this could not have been better. The contract
manager that I blamed for my punishment, rightly or wrongly,
had now departed from the depot in which I worked. This was
now the end of 2011, and the service was being delivered by
a new company, which represented a fresh start for me. No
longer would my misdemeanour be held against me. I could
now build a positive image of myself.

In order to find out if education was the right thing for me
to do to advance my career, or even if it was possible for me
to achieve, it was time to change. I had to change from being
unable to share my planned development with others as I now
needed information that was unavailable otherwise.

My first port of call was family as I had easy access to them
and felt less nervous so could therefore speak openly. As far as
I was aware, my two brothers both had good, professional jobs.
One was an accountant and the other worked in hospitality.
Two jobs that were certainly not a direct promotion from a
street cleansing operative, and therefore in my mind, must
have required some form of education. I was not wrong in
my assessment. As I came to learn, my two brothers had
both studied to achieve their current job roles, something
that I immediately had admiration for. I could, however, not
understand why I had not noticed this before, especially since I

started looking at how I could progress my career.

The reason I had not noticed was actually quite simple. We had never discussed education before. This was not a subject that was engaged during family quizzes, birthdays, weddings, or other such events. Reflecting on this, it was evident that talking about, or showing off about, educational development was not 'cool' within our family circle. We'd much rather talk about sport and make fun of each other at every opportunity. This had to change for me. I had to start educational conversations with my brothers.

I decided to call my brothers on the phone over the next few weeks and try to gain some information about their personal educational journeys. The findings were very similar from both of them. They had both decided that, after finding their initial full-time employment, they were not satisfied with their respective roles. From this, they decided to complete educational courses, related to accountancy for one brother and hospitality for the other, which progressed their careers quickly. This led to promotions, pay increases, and better working benefits.

The financial gain was of course a motivation for my development too, as I am sure it will be to you also. I believe it to be true that we can all want more money and, at times, be jealous of what others have. I do remember the very moment that one brother revealed to me, unintentionally, what he was earning annually. Now, this was not premier league footballer wages, but it was three times my annual salary. I could not believe it but knew that it was true as there was no need for my brother to lie to me and he had material things that I didn't.

Surprisingly, my first emotion was not jealousy. Looking back, I maybe should have been jealous, as this is also what I wanted, but it was not. Neither was it envy. I was totally happy with my brother being successful, especially financially. My first emotion was actually happiness. Happy that this is achievable for someone like me. In fact, someone very much like me, my brother. Someone that had the exact same schooling as me, grew up in the same house as me, had a similar friend group as me, and the same family as me. This was now confirmed, I can do it. This meant that I could now explore educational discussions outside of my family, and with the confidence that I am capable too of progressing my career.

My first educational discussion with somebody outside of my family came out of the blue and could not have been prepared for. My sporting hobby at the time was weight training in a gym within my hometown. The gym was full of different sorts of people, training for a multitude of different reasons, rugby, personal wellbeing, boxing, to name just a few. Not the place that I expected to find an educational discussion. Well, I was wrong.

I remember getting ready for my part-time training partner, a very competent power lifter, to spot me with a bench press set and the subject of his job arose. I cannot recall his actual job title, but it was in information technology (IT). I knew at the time that this was the perfect opportunity for me to ask, "did you study for that?". His response amazed me "yes, I completed a degree at university". Wow, this prompted so many more questions. It must have taken ten minutes before I started my bench press set. The answers were worth it though.

I found out that he had completed a foundation degree in an IT related subject, for which he had studied three years to achieve. I had no idea if, or how, the degree had progressed his career for good or bad. He did, however, still work within the IT sector, so I assumed that at least the degree did not deter him from continuing within his chosen industry. This at least was positive as it demonstrated that benefit can be gained from education. And considering this was the first time I held such a talk with a friend, I think that my questioning was actually rather good, even if a little intense. Intense only because I was super interested and wanted to capitalise on the opportunity.

I needed to act quickly on this new information. I knew that the IT sector had an educational route that appeared to aid a career, but it was not for me. I wondered if this was the same for the occupational area in which I was interested, supervision and management in street cleansing.

My first action was to search the websites of colleges within the city boundaries. I was personally aware of two and these would be viewed with great intent. I was pleased with my findings. Firstly, these websites were very easy to navigate, which was helpful considering my weak IT skills at the time, and secondly, the prices were affordable, even for my low wages at the time. Seeing that I did not know what to expect, this made my mind up. I was going to pick one and start.

In early 2012, I picked a leadership and management course at a local college. I had no idea of course length or study volume as these were not the aspects of the course that I was interested in, which I actually did not even read. My mind was made up by the 'level 5' status of this course. This was not entry level, and I knew that it would be immensely challenging for me. However, due to my lack of previous relevant qualifications, I had to undergo a course entry interview.

In all honesty, such an interview would have terrified me before I decided to develop myself. I cannot tell you how this changed but it did. This was an interview that I was actually looking forward to and prepared for. I made sure that I even had my GCSE qualifications available, although these were nearly twelve years old at this point and not particularly impressive. It transpired that the lady I met, who would become my teacher for the next two courses, was not interested in GCSE grades, or other specific qualifications that I did not have. The teacher wanted to know how committed I appeared to be and whether or not I would be able to complete the course. I clearly showed this commitment as I was offered a place on the course. I was delighted and could not wait to tell my wife and son the good news.

It was during the interview that the full extent of the challenge became known to me. This was a level 5 certificate that was assessed through submission of multiple essays (the certificate is one above the level 5 award and one below the level 5 diploma). The teaching was delivered in person at the college on Tuesday and Thursday evenings between 6pm and 9pm, which required me to leave home at around 5pm and would not return home until after 9:30pm. These were challenges that I was willing to accept without question. I was fully supported by my wife, which was encouraging as she clearly believed that I could do it. I paid the course fee, which was pleasantly far less than I had thought it would be, and got ready to start.

This was not a degree and probably wasn't going to impress many people, but for me this was the beginning of something great. I was honestly not interested in what other people thought of my journey at this point as I had taken the leap into education, and I was proud of it. Leadership and management were going to be my thing. I was twenty-seven years old and at the very start of my educational journey. You are never too old to start your journey.

Foundation Principe 2 – Locate the Ladder

Job Titles – *Your job title does not define you within your organisation. The same job title can mean many different things and have many different responsibilities.*

Your Place in the Company – *Don't be fooled that you cannot progress. Once you know where in the company you are you can observe those above you.*

The 'Perks' – *These are not reasons for progression, they are false signs of success.*

Education Works – *Education progresses careers. Look around you at successful people and assess whether education has helped them.*

Chapter 4

Principle 3 – Make the First Step

Step outside of your comfort zone

The first day of college arrived and I was excited, and understandably slightly nervous. I was stepping well and truly outside of my comfort zone. My comfort zone was turning up for work to sweep a street that I was familiar with, using tools I was familiar with, and answering questions that I was familiar with. A college environment was something that I most certainly was not familiar with. The time to question what this unknown scenario would present was over as day one was about to begin.

The first class took place on a Tuesday evening. The brief was to arrive ten minutes early to be able to park and locate the classroom. Due to my concern for being late I arrived at around 4pm, nearly two hours early. This was made possible as I had taken the day as annual leave from work to spend the entire morning preparing. I was at this point in my development not used to preparing for learning, but I did what I thought would assist me. I searched the internet extensively for articles relating to leadership and management. As I remember, I did not take any notes or print any content. I simply allowed myself to digest the new information and terminology.

In hindsight, none of this preparation was actually necessary for the first lesson as no specific learning took place. I arrived at the classroom and was greeted very kindly by the lady teacher who I had become acquainted with at the entry interview. On entering the classroom I made the conscious decision to sit at the front of the class. This was different from my school years when sitting at the front of the class was a last resort. But, this was different, it was the new educational me. I was paying to be at this class, and I wanted to learn everything that I could.

Not long after I was seated, ten minutes before class start time, other students began to arrive. They looked slightly nervous as I am sure I did. This course was clearly a big step for all of us and the faces that I saw in this day I was going to see many more times throughout the duration of the course. Thankfully, all of students appeared professional and willing to learn, with not one of them looking as if they were there to mess around. This was clearly the learning environment that I sought. I was not going to be disappointed.

The real course began, and I can honestly say that my world expanded. I was learning and writing about ideas and theories that were completely alien to me. It was continually fascinating that there was so much that I did not know. Not just me, but the other students too. This was a learning environment in which I felt from the very beginning that I belonged. The energy in the classroom was motivating and the discussions during coffee breaks even focused on the course material. I could not wait to return to each evening classroom session.

I did however still have a full time day job but now as a street cleansing driver team leader. This was not a promotion due to my studying, but the pay increase did contribute to paying the study fees. The new role did not allow me the thinking time that the street sweeper role did, as I had to concentrate on driving a vehicle, it did however make me a leader of a team. This assisted with my development as the words team and leader were familiar to me from my evening classes at the college. Now I could exercise what I was learning.

I made efforts outside of work to also progress my learning of my chosen subject area. An example of this relating to my physical hobby, the gym. I came to realise that I was spending three hours per week in the gym and as I was mostly cycling on a static bike my eyes were free for reading. This meant that I could exercise physically and mentally. I could read my educational documents even more and be better prepared for the next lesson. Perfect. This of course prompted some strange looks from other gym goers, although interestingly, not one person questioned what I was reading. Maybe they thought it was fiction, or maybe they just didn't care. It didn't bother me either way.

Of course, reading in this way was not as effective as if I was relaxed on a comfy chair with adequate lighting and a warm drink to sip on. I was on a bike, breathing heavy and sweating in a mildly lit room. That did not matter to me though as reading the material was more important. For this I needed to develop a reading approach. I decided to take only three items to read and concentrate on finishing them. I was aware that I would probably return to read the content again some other time and so I therefore focused on scanning the material. I did this by reading rather quickly and slowing down at any relevant points in the text. This ensured that my time on the exercise bike was useful. It is really important to not overthink this reading method as you will learn quickly which material to return to if you need to read it in greater depth. Moreover, you will also learn which material does not offer value to your study, thus saving time by not reading useless documents.

This approach was not one that I had been shown, it was one that I made up for yourself. It may not have been the most efficient use of my time, however, in that moment it kept me focused on my quest for education. And it was starting to pay off.

Challenge yourself

My educational focus helped in another way too. I was no longer concerned at all by any comments made to me by my colleagues. The most common comment would be that I was "wasting my time studying as you will not progress in the company". This could not have been more wrong. My time for progression arrived and it was directed related to my personal development with education.

These negative comments were no more prevalent than within my team at the time. As a street cleansing driver team leader I had two street cleansing operatives. The two that I had were older gentlemen with very strong negative views of not just the company, but the entire world. This included any ambition that anyone would have to succeed. They made it very clear to me that I had "no chance" with whatever I wanted to do. Sadly this was aired daily. Gladfully it became so predictable that it became humorous to me. That said, I was still eager to move away from this situation as soon as I could, and didn't have to wait long for an opportunity.

As the company under which I had the twelve month punishment had now departed, the operational approach changed. This change involved a larger element of supervision, which required employing more people as supervisors. Once I learned this I had zero hesitation. I was going to apply as soon as I could.

This application was the first time that I would be able to benefit from my newly acquired education. There was a section on the application form titled 'skills and education'. This is a section that I would have overlooked in years past as I did not have anything to write. Now, however, I did have. This made me smile. I remember spending a lot of time completing this section of the form. In fact, it took me three attempts as it had to be perfect. I detailed everything that I could from my level 5 certificate in leadership and management course and that I was already planning to complete the level 5 diploma in the following year.

I can only assume that this section of my application was impressive as it progressed me through to the interview stage. The process was thankfully very fast. It took only one week for the interviews to be arranged which did not leave too much time for me to overthink it. When my time came I was delighted to realise that I was going to be interviewed by two people that I had not met before. This gave me the opportunity to give a positive first impression, instead of any outcome potentially being predetermined by somebody that already knew me, and my past disciplinary history.

Along with being able to further discuss my studies within the interview, I could utilise the terminology that I had become accustomed to twice a week in the classroom at college which enabled me to communicate professionally with the two interviewers. I really enjoyed the interview and had a good feeling about getting the job. That said, one of the questions that they asked did raise a slight concern in myself. The question was surrounding how I would react to "crossing the counter". To explain, if I got the job I would no longer be a member of the front-line workforce but a supervisor that would need to enforce the rules within the company. This change was not something that I had experienced before and therefore I did not know exactly how I would react. I did however know that I wanted the promotion above anything else and that I would make any such transition work. I would need to challenge myself in this situation.

Again, the interview process moved very quickly. Only two days following my interview I was driving my cleansing route with my team of two street cleansing operatives when my phone rang. I pulled over to take the call which was from one of the interviewers who wanted to come and meet me on my route. Of course, I arranged to meet immediately. This was it, the moment I was waiting for. Success. I was offered the role on the spot and told that my recent personal development was a key reason for me getting the job. I accepted the offer and was now a street cleansing supervisor. I was very proud.

I received a new contract with a significant pay increase and was introduced to the management team as a supervisor. I took the contract home to show my wife and we celebrated with a lovely meal. To me, this promotion was also a way to say thank you to my wife for the support she continually showed me during my twelve month punishment period. We could now afford some of the things that we had not allowed ourselves in recent times. The financial improvement was a great relief. So much so, that I had to get out of bed 2am that night to read the contract again as it seemed unbelievable, and I could not sleep due to the excitement.

In addition to this, I now had a company van in order to travel for work. Wow. I was really happy. Well, until it dawned on me that I needed to park it somewhere in my street where I lived. Parking was at a premium and it was not completely welcomed by our neighbours. I had no idea that company benefits also had a downside. This was true also with a company laptop. I was issued a nearly new laptop together with accessories in order to assist me with my work. At first, this again made me feel happiness, and a sense of importance. However, this was short lived. What I did not take into account was that I was now able to work anywhere in the world, and at any time of day. This meant that weekends were no longer free. I found myself working many times outside of my contracted working hours.

My first day as a supervisor was actually not as challenging as I expected. In fact, it ran smoothly, and I was not overwhelmed at any point. One moment did however make me laugh. There was a street cleansing driver team leader that I had known for a few years up until this point. He was big, loud, and proud. He made a regular effort to tell people that he "says it how it is". This was true to a point as he offended many of my colleagues with his comments. He had also commented on what he thought of me only two weeks prior to my first day as supervisor. Needless to say that his opinion of me was not a nice one as I had showed interest in becoming a supervisor. Based on this, you may also be surprised that this individual was the first to offer me a cup of tea on my first day as supervisor. His behaviour changed immediately towards me; he could not have been nicer to me from this point forward.

This individual was not alone. I received constant attention from a certain group of people. The overtime people. These were the employees that were always wanting overtime to increase their pay packets. I had nothing against this want for extra working hours, it was actually very necessary to deliver the service. It was the tactics used by some to gain the extra hours that was interesting. Some would whisper to me so no one else could hear, some would try and find work that needed to be completed, and others would openly ask every single day. My task as supervisor was to ensure that the distribution of overtime was fair for all, and that only necessary work was allocated.

Something that I found to not be fair was the effort input by other supervisors, well, one in general. I learned a lot from this individual in a short period of time. A lot about what not to do. His approach was to be the best friend to every street cleansing operative, allowing them to come and do as they please, with no focus on company rules. This was alarming to me as my study module at the time was concentrated on operational compliance and organisational governance. In short, delivering an operation with integrity and efficiency. I was amazed not only that this supervisor was not aware of this, although in hindsight how would he be as he was not studying with me, but also the reaction of my operations manager when I raised my concern. No action whatsoever. Well, until the supervisor was dismissed for an unrelated issue.

There were other learnings to be had during this period through my own mistakes. I believe that there are certain situations that cannot be taught in a classroom. One of these was my very first time interviewing someone. I forget the exact position that I was interviewing for, but it was certainly a front-line operative role. This was a challenging proposition as it was a completely new experience, and I was worried that if I gave the person the role and they were not suitable it could be my fault. Furthermore their poor performance would lead to service failures and potential financial penalties. The stakes were high.

Thankfully, I was mentored in this situation by a very experienced human resources (HR) professional. The interview was also structured by a strict series of questions printed out on paper for us to follow. How can I go wrong? It seemed easy. It was, until the questions were finished and I decided to, for an unknown reason, improvise. I asked openly "how old are you?" and was swiftly interrupted by my mentor, informing me that I cannot ask this question. I felt very small in that interview room and did not know if I would ever get the chance to interview again. I knew at that time that I had lots of practical lessons to learn. I had to challenge myself further, and in as many different situations as I could.

Observe and learn

At this point I was well underway with my second year of leadership and management study, the level 5 diploma, at the same college and with the same teacher. I had successfully completed every assignment and maintained my desire to learn and develop. In fact there was never any doubt that I would continue by me or my teacher.

My observations continued. This time however I was dialled in on the next level, the operations management role. I must point out that although it has a different name from the manager that punished me, contract manager, it performed almost exactly the same duties. This was a role re-brand by the new company that now managed the contract. I was certain that this operations manager role, if it became available, would be achievable for me. That would require greater responsibility and decision making. But I was writing college papers about exactly that and was having related educational conversations with my fellow students at college on a twice-weekly basis.

I had a direct operations manager, to whom I reported. I had no idea about the previous experience of this manager, however, do think that she had a university degree, but I am not sure in what discipline. At this point I was not no longer in awe of people with a degree as I was thinking that soon I will have one too. Ok, I wasn't there yet, but I would be. This represented a positive mindset, one that was normal for me at this time in my development.

As I understood it at the time, the role of the operations manager was to enforce the policies and procedures if the supervisors were unable to do so, and support them however necessary to deliver the service to the desired standards. To achieve this, it was clear that the operations managers did not need to work as many hours as the supervisors. I did not know if this was a privilege, or it was a liberty taken by them. Either way, this was recognised by the front-line workforce as it was commented regularly that "the operations managers are on leave again for the morning". I don't know if I liked this assessment although I certainly did not defend it as a supervisor. To me it appeared to be true.

The main issue I had with the operations manager was the attitude when dealing with a tough situation, or any situation for that matter. My study up to this date had taught me to stay calm and consider options, all whilst treating every employee with respect and equal considerations. I did not always witness this. I witnessed first-hand how this manager had to become so angry in order to deliver a message to the group of supervisors. When I say angry, I mean angry. And this would be even to talk about something as insignificant as the request for new tools. It honestly took this person twenty minutes to calm down afterwards. It was astonishing. The message received by me was one of chaos. That said, this person was also very kind in certain circumstances and had a great sense of humour.

Part of me really enjoyed looking at this individual as I was continually surprised by how the actions regularly contradicted my leadership and management studies. An example coming with what could actually be considered a clever approach. The approach was to ascertain what concerns that the supervisors had during the daily meeting. The issue came when the supervisors started to name the concerns as the conversation was immediately ended by the operations manager, which became a frequent occurrence. I personally became annoyed that we, the supervisors, had to move away from our work for such a pointless outcome. Mainly because my studies taught me that if you ask a question you should be ready to listen to the answer, whatever that answer may be. Otherwise, don't ask the question. Our concerns as supervisors appeared irrelevant to the management team.

I, of course, was also observing the street cleansing operatives as I wanted to maximise performance. One such observation cannot be left out of this book as it still makes me laugh. I came to learn that you should always expect the unexpected, and that sometimes the unexpected is very funny. This was a Friday morning at 6:30am. Thirty minutes after the shift had begun and we, as a supervisory team, had become concerned about a street cleansing operative that had not reported for work, or rang in as sick, or otherwise. The call came in at around 7am from the employee and it was memorable. As explained by the employee, the reason that he did not attend work was that he lives on a farm and his bedroom window was open. The low morning fog entered his bedroom, and he could not see the alarm clock. My sense of humour was activated. I found this hilarious. This was a new one on me and still to this day the best lateness excuse I have heard.

My eyes were now on the next stage of my education as I had completed level 5, both certificate and diploma in two years. I had no plans to rest. Time to level up. I found and signed for a course at level 7 extended diploma in strategic management and leadership, equivalent to master's degree level study. Wow, this was a huge step for me. I was right, this is possible.

Foundation Principe 3 – Make the First Step

Step Outside of Your Comfort Zone – *You will need to utilise different situations in order to maintain your focus, not all of which will be within your comfort zone.*

Challenge Yourself – *Position yourself in situations that are new. Remember, your journey is different from that of other people, and you need to challenge yourself to succeed.*

Observe and Learn – *Learn from everything around you, good or bad. At this point you will make your own mind up and be able to judge the actions of others based on what you have already learned.*

Chapter 5

Principle 4 - Question Everything

Open your mind

The level 7 extended diploma in strategic management and leadership course was delivered in the classroom between 1pm – 9pm on Wednesday's and lasted nine months. This was a huge commitment but at this time for me there was no other way. This was not only the most expensive course that I had funded but also the most challenging.

I arrived on the first afternoon knowing that I would meet more professionally driven students than I had in previous years. I was not wrong. I was delighted to meet with a pair of colleagues that worked for the fire service. They both welcomed me with a handshake and opened with questions about where I had studied up to this point. Of course, I could answer this comprehensively as I had studied non-stop for two years. Something that I was immensely proud of and not afraid to disclose to my new fellow students.

They also had come from a few years of studies, as did all the other students in the class. In fact, without such a student would not have been welcomed onto the course. I had to realise very quickly that this was a different level of study, far above what I had experienced previously. And also, that I had to be prepared for every lesson as all of the other students were and I did not want to be left behind.

This I did. I made sure that I used evenings and weekends to re-read any documents that we were provided and made additional efforts to look up more on the subjects that we were studying. I was convinced that this was a solid approach and was pushing me in the right direction. The proof however would be in the marking of our written assignments, of which there were nine in the duration of the course.

Well, was I in for a shock. I was certain that I was making considerable progress and actually placed myself near the top of the class, in my mind anyway. This was clearly not the case and I found out in a big way. I was led at home one Saturday morning with anticipation checking my emails for feedback from my first assignment submission. I was sure that I had produced a fine piece of work and wanted to set my weekend up nicely by reading positive feedback.

The email from my course lead landed early in my email inbox which meant that I did not have to wait any longer. I wish that I would not have checked. It was horrendous feedback for me and was even in red writing (never a good sign). I had rushed, I had not researched sufficiently, I had not referenced my readings, and so on. I was honestly completely devastated. I cried and did not speak to anyone for hours. I had to process this 'failure' in my mind. This however did not signify that I had failed the assignment it only required me to re-submit. Nevertheless, this was a huge setback in my mind. I had two choices. Give in or accept the feedback and improve.

When I arrived at class on the next Wednesday, I was delighted that the course lead mentioned nothing further regarding the feedback as I was expecting it to be read out in front of the class. It was as if it had not happened. Well, until I stayed behind and asked her. The response was much better than I could have ever envisaged. I was made aware that this is part of the process. You, as a student must 'open your mind' to knowledge and know that there is far too much to learn than is ever possible, but always continue to learn. Interestingly, or as I would like to think because of me, the course lead opened the next lesson with this 'open your mind' concept. This was not just fascinating for me but for all in attendance.

Our first learning in this lesson was enlightening and thought provoking. Simply put, it is a false assumption to think that the person sat next to you in a meeting knows something that you do not. This took some time to digest as at this point in my career I was attending some rather important meetings (in my opinion of course) and sat next to people with jobs that were considered greater than mine as a street cleansing supervisor. My teacher was telling me that these people actually did not necessarily know more than me. But they must because they earn more money, right? This was a revelation although is easily understood when you ask yourself a question: Do you know the actual meaning of each acronym that you use in your working life?

In my case the answer was a resounding no. Once I considered all of the SLA's, KPI's, PDA's, and RTA's (to name just a few) that I used in conversation daily, I realised that I did not know what they all actually meant. It dawned on me at this moment that I too would appear to others to know more than I really did. A position that I was uncomfortable with. Not because I cared that people thought that I did not know things, but because I was uncomfortable talking about things that I did not truly understand. In essence, I was representing what I had come to believe of 'bad' managers, saying without knowing. Which raised a further question that opened my mind, how are managers in their positions?

This aligned perfectly with another lesson taught to me, and my fellow class colleagues, by my level 7 course leader, "if you don't ask and learn, how will you progress?". So, it felt right to explore this in greater detail, paying particular attention to its relation to management figures that I was dealing with day in day out, in an operational environment.

It appeared clear to me that education did not even register on the radar of the managers to which I was reporting. It was as if they had reached their respective pinnacles and knew everything that they needed to in order to hold their prestigious positions within the organisation. As a supervisor I was privy to what they did not seem to be, a true reflection of what the workforce thought of them, purely autocratic. By this I mean that the workforce believed that the managers held absolute power and were unwilling to consider other people's opinions.

I could not contest this assumption myself as I was experiencing similar. Certainly not what the textbooks or lectures were telling me were good individual, or team, traits when wanting to build teams to achieve consistently good outcomes. Quite honestly, this only made the job of a street cleansing supervisor more difficult. It did not seem right to me. It was difficult for me to comprehend how my managers remained in their positions. Well, these were my opinions anyway.

Of course, I was viewing the situation through an educational lens. I was judging every decision, action, and instruction, based on academic concepts that I was studying in the college classroom. Furthermore, I was measuring my managers against my fellow students, all of which were at least at middle management level. This was possibly biased as I held nothing but admiration for my classmates as they were opening their minds to new ideas, whilst being willing to question everything around them. Values that I was also beginning to use in my life. While at the same time I was constantly questioning the values held by my managers within the workplace. I could certainly see how they would benefit from progressing their education, however, did not see any sign of that happening. Even so, they were very 'safe' in their job roles.

Being 'safe' in my job role was not an objective of mine in any guise. I wanted to be the best I could be within the organisation and knew that I could achieve this through opening my mind to education and new ideas. Honestly, there was not one point in my development that education hindered my progress. It only pushed me forward.

Judge your surroundings

My constant questioning of what was happening around me was in full flow. This does not mean that I was stopping people mid-sentence to question and challenge what they were saying. Nor does it mean that I was always stopping actions of individuals when I was uncertain with what they were doing. I was questioning things to myself and trying to process in my mind whether or not it was correct. I am fully aware that my judgements were not, and are still not, always right. The important point is that I was not accepting things just because that is the way they are always done. An approach which aligned with the teachings of my level 7 course lead, to question everything.

Some judgements are exceedingly difficult to make and take a lot of time to decipher what you have observed. Some are not so difficult. A fine example of this came during my time as a street cleansing supervisor when I was reporting into two operations managers. This was a prosperous period in my career within this specific street cleansing depot as we were delivering a good service and achieving commendable external survey results. This did however not result in a harmonious workplace. Quite the opposite in fact.

What we became used to as supervisors was a passive aggressive approach from the operations managers in that they regularly displayed indirect hostility towards us. This surprised me as the literature that I was reading for my management and leadership studies at no point suggested that this is appropriate behaviour. This passive aggressive approach not only seemed premediated, but also seemed to be enjoyed by both operations managers. The supervisors did certainly not enjoy it. It made for an extremely uncomfortable environment.

An example of this relates specifically to email communication. We would regularly have operational meetings with all managers and supervisors in attendance. There was no detailed agenda, although they did seem to be beneficial to the service as issues were debated and solutions very often found and implemented. That said, no supervisors really felt comfortable speaking out, for a reason that still frustrates me to this day. One of the operations managers would be very complimentary during the meeting, in agreement with most solutions. However, on multiple occasions this manager would leave the meeting when it finished and send a scathing email criticising something that was considered fine in the meeting that had occurred only minutes before. This whilst copying in the organisation's directors. Clearly only for self-promotion and sending a message to the directors that strong management was in force.

I began to question the reasoning behind this in greater detail and concluded that it was power that was behind these actions. I was sure that I did not want to use any power in this way as I did not want anyone to feel the way that I did. I therefore pledged to myself that I must always make every effort to use any management power for positive purposes only, not for self-promotion.

Making this pledge was a clear indication to me that building judgements about your surroundings can improve your own behaviour. Certainly, a viable reason to continually judge your surroundings. Irrelevant of whether you consider your findings to be good or bad you will improve. Considering this, I hold no hard feelings towards the operations managers that I reported to during this time. In fact, I thank them as they taught me many lessons, most of which were learned following my observations of their management styles, and associated approaches.

Work towards your goals

The work I was putting in as a supervisor started to get recognition, possibly because both operations managers left the business. This presented the opportunity to step up, an opportunity that I was not going to let pass by me if I could help it. Thankfully, the decision was made by the organisation to appoint two interim operations managers, of which I was chosen as one thereof. I guess the company wanted to see how the new interims would get on before confirming in the posts permanently. Either way, it was an interim promotion that I accredited to my recent education. On reflection, they would not have appointed me in this new role if I were still sweeping the streets, would they? The work I was putting in was progressing me towards my goals.

The interim promotion was extremely uplifting and rewarding, but at this time in my development I wanted to use my newly acquired skills for direct personal benefit too. Initially I had no idea in which form this would be or whether it would be a positive outcome, but I wanted to try something.

My studies at this point focused on financial planning. This related to me personally as I with my wife, like many others, had a mortgage, alongside many other financial commitments and monthly expenditure. Up to this point I had never considered that I could treat my own finances in the same way that I was learning how to manage business accounts. I decided that I would work towards paying off our mortgage by using these newly acquired skills, as mortgage payments are a constant drain on income. This was only going to get worse for us as interest rates were rising and we were due to fix the mortgage rates for another five years within the next twelve months. Therefore, our monthly payment was due to increase.

Of course, I knew that I would not pay the mortgage off overnight. This was going to be a long -term goal. My first step was to ascertain exactly how much was left to pay on the mortgage and what the monthly cost was. It sounds crazy to me now that I did not know this information, but previously I never really considered it. It was from these figures that I proceeded to plan how I would expediate the payback speed. For which I needed to develop a financial payback model that would enable this.

I cannot over-complicate this financial model for you, as the process was actually rather simple and very effective. I started by creating a spreadsheet to document all of our income and expenditure. It was really important not to leave anything out. I had to include gym memberships, mobile phones subscriptions, as well as food sopping and all other expenses. I gathered this data by looking at the previous month's bank statements and receipts to ensure that my data was accurate.

The task was now to enter all of the data into the spreadsheet, which enabled me to work some calculations. First off, I compared our monthly expenditure against the monthly wage income from my wife and me. I found that if we stuck to the financial model (budget) we would have money left over. Not a substantial amount of money, but money, nonetheless. Money that could be used to work towards the goal by paying additional sums off of our mortgage.

The second calculations were made on the back of this. I wanted to know what the maximum money I could allocate per month to over-pay our mortgage, and how much quicker could our mortgage be finished. Again, this was entered into a spreadsheet to document the figures, but in this case, it was also used to forecast the outcomes. This spreadsheet could be altered, if an additional mortgage payment was made or a payment could not be made, to deliver amended mortgage end date. This was truly effective. I used to constantly monitor the progress within the spreadsheet as the mortgage term reduced over time, which was extremely motivating and kept me on track. The overall result was a twelve-year mortgage term reduction. Yes, during this period we probably did not have too much spare cash for finer things. But we avoided twelve years of mortgage interest payments, achieved by what I had learned from my studies.

Of course, my focus also remained on my aim for progression within my career. I was very proud of the interim operations manager role that I was carrying out, but my mind was continuously on the next promotion. I was comfortable with this outlook as I thought that my studies were developing me into an educated manager. By this I mean that I was looking at management processes using theory within a teaching environment. I believe that this improves a manager's capabilities as it is teaching management principles that are proven, rather than simply gaining experience 'on the job' and relying on guidance from their managers. This may not be everybody's view of this situation, but it is mine.

Thankfully, very soon after becoming an interim operations manager, the organisation decided to make one of the posts (remember there were two) permanent. Music to my ears. I did of course apply for this role as soon as I was able. The application process was not lengthy at all. As I remember, from advertisement through to appointment was only four weeks.

It was not surprising that the competition that I had for this role was from the other interim operations manager. This individual was very experienced within the street cleansing department and was actually my supervisor during my twelve-month punishment period. It was during this time that I grew fond of this person as he was reasonably kind to me, well not deliberately rude as others had been. Furthermore, he appeared to me to be a good interim operations manager and had the respect of the street cleansing operatives.

We had both passed the psychometric test and were progressed as the only two into the final stage, the face-to-face interview. Deep down, I knew that I had little to no chance of success in securing this promotion. My competition was far more experienced than me and had proven himself within the organisation. Even so, I was really looking forward to the interview as it was a chance to exercise my interview skills, not something that comes around very often.

The interview itself was tough, although I was strangely not nervous before or during. My studies up to this point had certainly not prepared me for this environment, as the questioning was very industry specific. I remember being bemused by one question relating to street cleansing innovation. I had no answer but did remain calm. Although this was embarrassing for me at the time, it was a very good lesson and has guided me to ensure that I fully research all potential questions before any future interview.

As expected, I was unsuccessful in this interview. The role was awarded to my competitor, which was the right decision if I am honest. I was really pleased for him while at the same time disappointed in every way. That said, I was also proud that I had put myself in the position of getting the promotion. This enhanced my confidence in my ability even further and provided me with a valuable experience. I was hoping that my profile within the organisation was now raised. I may not be the operations manager, but I was second choice. This was certainly progress towards my goal of developing myself.

To my delight, my disappointment did not last very long at all. My effort for the job was not in vain. I had returned to my interim position with energy and determination and within a few months the organisation had decided to make the other interim operations manager role permanent. Following a brief meeting with a company senior manager, I was made aware of my appointment as a fully pledged street cleansing operations manager. This was a huge step for me. I could now use the title 'manager' for the first time legitimately, and without needing to precede it with interim.

It was very clear to me that had I not tried to get the position the first time around I would not have been automatically selected for the second operations manager role. This is proof that failure should not stop you. You must continue in aim to achieve your goals. This is what I did, and it paid off. I worked constantly towards my goals.

Foundation Principe 4 – Question Everything

Open Your Mind *– New ideas and education will expand your knowledge in your subject area. There is more to learn than you can ever know.*

Judge Your Surroundings *– Your own performance and behaviour will improve by judging the actions of others. Trust your judgements if they are factually based.*

Work Towards Your Goals *– The effort you put in may not deliver immediate results, but rest assured that they will be noticed by others and will likely provide benefits later on.*

Foundation principle 4 concludes the first section of this book, which will now progress onto the second section, the elite principles. By following the foundation principles, you will already have a solid purpose for learning, know your place in your organisation, have taken your first step in your development, and be willing to question everything around you. This is an exciting start and positions you well to maximise your potential.

Chapter 6

Principle 5 - Try New Vocabulary

The second section of this book sets out the 4 elite principles, which contains experiences that I had from being an operations manager through to regional manager, and also a university lecturer. Having followed the 4 foundation principles, you will be well set to take your development to the next level, the Elite Level.

Taking it to the next level

Being an operations manager gave me additional confidence within the classroom. Especially considering that all of the other students were managers before commencing the level 7 course. I was now able to engage in management discussions by opening with "as a manager, I…". Very different from "if I was a manager, I think I would…". My opinion was now relevant in the academic discussions, and I had real-life significant examples to draw upon.

This however did not signify that I had reached my potential, in fact it was at this time that I was made aware of how little I actually knew. Opening my mind, as discussed in foundation principle 4, was a good start, but the next lesson taught by the level 7 course lead was astonishingly impactful but easy to grasp. This particular teacher always found innovative ways to challenge us, and this was no different.

We all arrived on early Wednesday afternoon, as every week, and were greeted by a single question, "what is spelunking?". This was completely unexpected. We were given a couple of minutes to think and then write our answers down on a piece of paper. I had no idea whatsoever and decided to hazard a guess with it being a medieval dance if I remember correctly. No surprise to me at the time that I was far from the mark. I felt quite silly really but shouldn't of as out of the twelve students present only one knew the correct answer, the exploration of caves. Well, the answer given was potholing, but close enough and accepted by the course lead.

The purpose of the exercise was to demonstrate that people do not understand all words. Moreover, that people will read articles, journals, reports, newspapers, and other written documents whilst not stopping to recognise words that are not known. It was then explained to us students that if words are not understood the true meaning of the writing cannot be really appreciated as it is intended. Therefore, we could be missing the important points throughout our reading. This was pertinent to us as we were reading multiple academic papers per week in order to research for our own written assignments, and so needed to make sure that we took everything from our reading that we could. To help with this the course lead set us a challenge.

It was suggested that we purchase the financial times and set about reading it from front to back, whilst highlighting every word that we did not understand the meaning of. I thought this would be easy as I was a few years into my educational journey and an operations manager. Very wrong indeed. In fact, it was quite a confidence knock, but a lesson very well served.

The very next day I brought the financial times (for the first time in my life) and commenced reading it as suggested. Me, and my yellow highlighter pen, began marking every word that I did not understand. Honestly, the very first page contained over twenty words that were alien to me. I was amazed. How could this be? And so, I continued onto the second page with very similar results. The biggest surprise however was the amount of time that this process was taking. I calculated that it would have taken more than five hours to finish the newspaper. I decided that the point was proven and stopped. I needed to now address this. I could not go on not understanding my readings.

I was realistic as I accepted that I would not be able to learn every word in the English dictionary, which would be a step too far. But I could attempt to know the words used within my industry and those associated with management and leadership, which of course was my educational focus. The way I went about this was to develop a means by which to record and learn the words that I did not understand during conversation.

I was now involved in many meetings at management level and as such had frequent opportunities to listen to new vocabulary and industry specific acronyms. To keep track of what I was hearing, and therefore what I needed to learn, I developed the 'bottom page line' concept. A simple, but at the same time, extremely effective, way to learn.

I realised that at certain times in meetings, or the classroom, the opportunity will arise that will enable me to verbally ask for an explanation of something I did not understand. However, these opportunities were not always available and constantly disrupting someone for an explanation is not helpful. Therefore, I drew a line straight across every page that I was making notes on, roughly two inches from the bottom, in order to document words, acronyms, terms, or anything else that I did not understand.

It was down to me to return to these points after the meeting or college lesson and make every effort to understand them. I did this every time, and honestly still do it today. The benefits that you gain cannot be overstated. Based on my finding in foundation principle 4, that people make the false assumption that the person next to you knows more than you, it is likely that the points that you make using the 'bottom page line' concept contain items are also not known by the person sat next to you. The difference being that by the time the next meeting or lesson comes around you would have progressed your knowledge of the specific points that you did not know. You therefore are starting to know more than others, taking your education to the next level.

To maximise the effectiveness of this concept I made sure that I dedicated time to learn the points. I would make cards with them written on to carry around with me and take every available opportunity to read them and even ask my wife and son to test me. I wanted to know the points completely by memory and be able to use them in conversation. This quest led to many interesting meetings.

I knew at this point in my education that I was willing to question everything around me and had no issue with making it known that I did not understand something. I did however not know whether the managers and directors above me in the organisational chart would also be willing to question something. I really expected them to given their statuses in the company. They did, but not so often.

I decided to test the water by using words that I did not think others knew, of course I could not have been certain that they did not know but made the assumption anyway. In order to maximise the effectiveness of the test I focused on words that I had never heard them use themselves. I clearly remember the word that I wanted to use, as it was one that I had noted (bottom page line) in the classroom during the previous week. The word was 'ubiquitous' and when I first heard it I had absolutely no idea what it was. It could have been another word for potholing for all I knew, just like spelunking. The word actually means appearing, or found, everywhere. The challenge was now to learn it and apply it in conversation.

I spent the weekend practicing the word, not continuously, but whenever I had chance. I must have made up at least ten different variations of it and really struggled to pronounce the word correctly. This was without trying to use the word within a sentence. I remember not sleeping very well on the Sunday night ahead of the Monday morning operations meeting, as this was the stage that I had set to test my belief that no-one would question the meaning of the word. These kinds of words were not commonplace at this meeting, and I could not think of a better audience, as it was confirmed that it would be attended by my managers and directors. I am aware that it may sound like I was showing off, but that could not be further from the truth as I had spent a considerable amount of time learning it. This was an outcome of my efforts.

The Monday morning meeting was about to start at 10:00am and I had already practiced the word at least thirty times, ten of which I am sure I still pronounced incorrectly. Confidence was low going into this, considering also that I had a job to do within the meeting. I had to make sure that I achieved what I needed for my team from the meeting and could not just concentrate on the test. That said, I spent the first five minutes of the meeting practising in my head and had not listened to a word that had been spoken. Eventually my time came. I started talking about resource management and how it was "ubiquitous" that paperwork was below standard. I delivered the word perfectly with a professional demeanour, and awaited the response, if there was one.

There was, and it absolutely confirmed my belief. A director amazed me with his response, "don't use words like that on a Monday". To me it was a sign that he did not understand the word and was even possibly threatened by my education. Well even if he was not, it grew my confidence within that particular environment. I flourished thereafter in the meeting, progressing the ideas that I raised.

I do not encourage this technique at each meeting that you attend, as I am sure that your colleagues will become annoyed by not being able to understand what you are saying. I suggest however that you should raise your level and not settle to the standard around you. Improving your vocabulary is a way of doing this. For instance, 'ubiquitous' is a word that I now use in conversation without thinking, which has advanced my vocabulary.

Don't settle for half measures

Learning singular words or acronyms does not always learn, or achieve, what is necessary. Simply entering a sophisticated word into a sentence will earn a certain level of respect, granted, but it does not necessarily expand your knowledge on a particular subject. To achieve this, a greater level of focus is required. Taking your education again further. In order to do this, you will need to identify a word that holds significant value to you. By value I mean that learning it will increase your subject knowledge within a desired situation.

I have two specific examples of when this particular learning technique has benefited me, and the company that I worked for, in real professional environments. The first came before a final tender interview, when we (the company that I represented at the time) were given the opportunity to sell our service offering and explain how we would be better than our competitors. This was by far the biggest such meeting that I had been involved in and wanted to make a positive impression.

I remember being in a well-known branded coffee shop in central London two hours before the meeting and being informed that I would be leading the presentation slide focused on governance. Ideally, this would have been discussed before the day of the meeting, but to the honest, our team had truly little preparation time and were actually very proud of the presentation that we had produced. This was not the time to question the decision to allocate me the slide, rather the time to learn as much as I could about the subject before the meeting. I knew that two hours was not long enough to perfect my understanding, but my approach proves that an understanding can be achieved, or at least an understanding can be portrayed to others.

My approach was simple. I searched the word 'governance' on my phone. Yes, that simple. This was my first attempt at such an exercise and so I had to make it up. Once I read the understanding of the word, I spent at least five minutes running the definition over and over, simplifying it as I went. This didn't seem onerous as I was used to practicing single words regularly. The final explanation that I decided on was that governance was 'the managing of interactions and decision making.' Whether this was 100% accurate or not, it made sense to me and would be what I would take into the meeting.

The meeting started well, considering that we were presenting for a panel of twelve people, ten of which I had never seen before. I had however not contributed really to the proceedings in the first thirty minutes. Probably because I was focused on remembering my new learning, and because these were the presentation slides not allocated to me. Thankfully, the time came in the meeting for the governance slide, and therefore my opportunity to talk.

I opened up exactly as I had hoped. "As per the definition, we have considered all governance on the contract with managing the interactions and decision making…". I took a breath and very quickly observed the room. It was clear that all accepted this statement, with zero visual responses that seemed to me to question my understanding of the subject. In fact, the sales manager, whom I had only met once prior to the meeting, appeared to be impressed, making a distinctive head nod in my direction. Wow. This worked. It then allowed me a room full of people that would then listen to me talk about the subject. Mission achieved by taking time to learn something at short notice, not necessarily by being a subject expert. I am not saying that our success was dependant on my explanation of governance, but we did win the contract and I certainly contributed towards that.

The second time that I remember intentionally learning an explanation in order to further my understanding came at around about the same time, but in different circumstances. This time it was classroom based and very much related to the level 7 strategic management and leadership course. The term that was new to me was corporate strategy. Initially, I could not have explained this term and had certainly never used it in a sentence, let alone talked about it at length. Considering that the word strategy formed part of the course name, I thought that learning it can only help me with my study. I was right.

This challenge needed to be embraced with full effort as the explanation was very long, and as such difficult to remember. I decided to also reword it slightly in order to increase my chance of memorising it. I produced explaining corporate strategy as:

"The direction and scope of an organisation over the long term within a competitive environment to achieve advantage through configuration of resources in order to meet market needs and reach or exceed stakeholder expectations."

A mouthful for sure and with multiple grammatical errors. But this was not important. What was important was that I was able to learn it, and more importantly, able to talk about it in detail. To achieve this, I enlisted the help of my Son, Stanley, who was six years of age at the time. You may ask why I did this. I cannot say to be honest. I was making it up as I went along, as I had no guidance on such a matter. Of course, I did not expect Stanley to be able to, or even want to, speak about corporate strategy with anyone else. In hindsight I probably just wanted to be accountable to him for learning it. And it worked.

I had printed the explanation on pieces of A4 paper and placed them around our house (again supported by my wife as she did never ask me to remove them). From this I made sure that every time I passed by one of the pieces of paper I would stop and practice out loud. Interestingly, this did not take too long for me to learn, and Stanley also once managed to recite it verbatim. It amazed me how easy it was to learn, although the proof of this learning would be to use the term in a working or academic environment. The time came very soon afterwards.

The level 7 course was progressing well, and we were regularly introduced to new teachers that were teaching their respective modules. As each teacher was introduced to the class, they naturally wanted to gauge the level of knowledge of the students, which went in my favour for this particular example. One certain teacher, employed to deliver the marketing module, provided me with the perfect opportunity to demonstrate my new learning, and yes, show off a little bit, although this was not my primary objective. He opened his first lesson by asking what corporate strategy was, as this formed a large part of the course. What! I could not believe my luck and raised my hand as quickly as I could, waving it around to make sure I was noticed. I was noticed, and immediately given the platform to deliver. I nailed the explanation perfectly and was greeted by the teacher with amazement and congratulations. I was extremely proud and remember the explanation to this day. Not only this, but I have also used it in many work meetings since. It always gives me silence from the attendees and allows me more time to elaborate on the subject.

You may be asking how you can use a specific explanation of a term more than once and not seem to be repeating yourself. You would be right to ask this question as that is not the intention. The intention is that you learn the explanation which enables you to expand on specifics. To explain, I set out my explanation of corporate strategy again:

"The direction and scope of an organisation over the long term within a competitive environment to achieve advantage through configuration of resources in order to meet market needs and reach or exceed stakeholder expectations."

For starters, you will notice that it mentions the direction and scope of an organisation at the beginning of the explanation. Therefore, when entering any discussion surrounding corporate strategy you should be considering this. For example, if the discussion was around the corporate strategy related to a specific organisation you would need to consider the organisation's direction, with could be their forecasted growth, and the organisation's scope, which may be explained by what services they provide and in what geographical regions of the UK. This may seem over-complicated or even superfluous, but I managed to learn this level of understanding by simply learning the explanation. Which you can do too for any term or explanation that you wish to learn.

I fully recommend learning such things to memory. You can gain a solid understanding of subject matters that others use without really knowing the true meaning. Don't settle for half measures, learn the full understanding.

Continue the challenge

In order to progress, you must continually challenge yourself. This can mean engaging in conversations with people not specifically knowledgeable with your subject interest or expertise. This, however, does not always work when starting these conversations on your own by trying to talk about your studies with your friends. You need to be aware of your audience, which I have learned to my embarrassment. I was once playing golf with a friend and wanted to talk about my studies between holes of a golf course. Naively, I thought he had been interested and so I continued. But, when I looked around, he was pretending to be asleep, which was not good as he was driving the golf buggy.

That said, times will present themselves for you to engage in conversations, whether that be in the workplace or classroom, which are alien to you. I suggest that you take these opportunities as you will be surprised with how well what you know will translate into our areas of knowledge. It will give you the chance to exercise your vocabulary and understandings from a different perspective, which is actually encouraged within the academic arena. Academic language does transfer across the fields, and you should not be afraid to try it.

I remember one such opportunity coming my way. I was on a train journey back from London on a very busy train during rush hour. I managed to get an aisle seat next to a well-dressed young man who was reading an academic paper. I couldn't resist and had to ask what he was reading, and possibly studying. As a fellow academic he had no issue sharing. He was studying some sort of insect related subject at PhD. level, far above my level 7. I must admit, I really enjoyed the conversation and was fascinated when he pulled a cardboard box from his bag. It contained multiple dead insects that he had loaned from a London based museum. I had never seen anything similar. I really do wonder what the couple behind us was thinking we were talking about. It probably disturbed their discussion about their shopping trip, but I didn't really care. I was learning. Although, I really can't remember anything about the insects if I am honest.

In fact, I was constantly learning. This was now certainly not something that I was going to give up. Although, I did not know what was next. The level 7 course had finished, and I had passed all of the modules. I celebrated with the family and was very proud. This was far above anything that I could have ever imagined I would achieve when I started the level 5 certificate some years earlier. But it was possible. My thoughts were no longer on the twelve months punishment that had initially fuelled my development, it was now on my next step to continue the challenge. I just needed to find the next step.

I found this in a way that I did not expect, as I had found to be the norm, rather than the exception. I was playing darts, yes darts, with my senior manager and thought I would drop the question into conversation. This individual had been a person that I had looked up to for a while due to his honest nature, which I thought would give me a true reflection of the situation.

The question I asked was simple, "what shall I study next to progress?". The answer was equally simple and amazingly fast coming, "MBA". As you will know by now, I asked what this meant. It was explained that this is the Master of administration, a master's degree usually studied by senior management and businesspeople. This sounded perfect. It was definitely not a qualification that anyone else that I knew had, which made it even more desirable.

There was however caution given. I was told that the management consultant that was working on our contract had been sponsored to complete an MBA, but decided to refuse the chance as it was too onerous and time consuming. I was concerned at this point as the management consultant appeared to be a very accomplished individual, and certainly someone that I had assumed to have qualifications greater than mine. At the same time, I had never been a master of anything. So, this would continue my challenge without doubt.

That was it, decision made. My mind was on studying to achieve an MBA. My time now had to be spent finding a suitable location to achieve this goal. I found this at the University of Gloucestershire, England, and I was certain that I would give everything that I needed to. I was continuing the challenge and knew deep down that this next stage in my development was only possible because of the education that I had developed up to this point.

Elite Principe 1 – Try New Vocabulary

Taking it to the Next Level – *Raise your own level and do not settle for any lower standard that you observe around you.*

Don't Settle for Half Measures – *Learn the full understanding of any terms that you use. You will develop an expert understanding of something relevant in your field.*

Continue the Challenge – *Appreciate your achievements and continue the challenge within further education.*

Chapter 7

Principle 6 - Do Something Every Day - No Matter How Small

Time to focus

My MBA journey began with a two-day introduction onto the course, whereas like the beginning of the level 7 course I met a classroom full of new people. It was very clear though that the concentration had intensified. These students were incredibly focused on what they wanted to achieve, having already spent many years getting to this position in their academic journeys. I felt comfortable in this environment as I too had reached this position.

Of all of my fellow students that I met over these two days, one individual stood out to me and furthered my desire to progress. This person was more senior in age that the rest of us and had already achieved higher study (DBA, Doctor of Business Administration). Which posed the question, why spend time on lower-level study? The answer given to me was that the individual had not completed an MBA and wanted to continue his academic journey. I loved this. I had admiration for this person in his continued pursuit to learn.

If this were not motivating enough, I remember vividly being amazed by the way that this person could communicate academically over the two days. I was constantly adding new words using my bottom page line technique. I must have taken away over ten words and terms to learn, from this person alone. But what was even more astonishing to me came when I was given the business card of the individual. I had never seen so many letters after someone's name. I was quite frankly speechless, and immediately wanted the same myself. It was very impressive to me and signified a consistent academic commitment.

I may not have had these letters after my name, but I was intensely focused, and my family and friends were starting to take note of my progression. Which to me was especially important as it gave me opportunities to talk about my studies with them. This was surprising to me as I did not think that anyone was noticing my development, and I was aware that my wife was always picked before me at the annual family quiz (I was quite often last pick to be honest, and still am today). However, I must have been doing something worth recognising. Although this was very encouraging to me, it was not the finish line. I could not rest on my achievements, I had to focus daily to ensure consistent progress.

To do this I had to find my best study time in the day. This may seem an insignificant consideration when progressing through your studies. I thought so too, in fact, it wasn't previously a consideration for me at all. Well, until during the MBA two-day introduction that was. One of the lecturers presented material relating to study practices and planning. The question was raised to the class, "what is your best study time?." The lecturer explained that he was completely alert first thing in the morning and therefore any academic material read at that time of day was learned more effectively, and as a result retained. Conversely, the lecturer confessed to not being suited to evening learning.

This resonated with me perfectly. This was the same as me, although I had never previously acknowledged it. Sub-consciously I had always gravitated to study first thing in the morning. I now knew that this was my preference and that was the same as at least one other academic. Which gave me confidence to continue with this approach. That said, please remember that in order to complete studies, like level 7 or MBA, evening study at times will be inevitable. Mainly due to the amount of study and writing required in order to succeed. Study efficiency should however be maximised whenever possible, which for me meant early mornings.

This was furthermore important for me as I worked full-time throughout all of my studies. Therefore, for me any annual leave that I took to attend university needed to provide the best output that it could. My approach to achieve this remained the same throughout my MBA study. I would arrive at the university library to start studying at 6:00am, this required a solid commitment as I lived forty-five minutes from the campus, which meant a pre 5:00am alarm call. I know from experience that my approach is not overly popular as it was common that no other students would arrive before 10:30am. Fine for me. I had the library to myself.

As soon as I entered the library, I would position myself at the desk that had become my usual spot, chosen for its proximity to the literature that was relevant to my study, and quiet location within the room. I had no interest in anything other than commencing my study immediately. I would set about gathering any literature that would assist me for the study session and pile them at my desk. Study was then underway, and it was effective every time. Of course, I had to take a break every now and again but did not want to lose focus, which is easy to do. To mitigate this possibility, I developed a walking route that took me to a quiet corridor with vast natural sunlight. This allowed me time to refresh and return to study in a timely manner without venturing too far from my studying location. This ensured that my focus did not stray far from the study.

Of course, study takes place away from the university library also. In fact, for me most of my studying for the MBA was not conducted at the university campus. Very rarely did I get the opportunity to attend as I needed to use annual leave or attend on the weekends. Time also used for family and friends. It was a juggling act to be honest. I had to capitalise on every spare moment for studying. This is the commitment required at master's level of study and one of the reasons that it is held in such high regard.

A favourite method of mine was to use travel to my advantage. I found that carrying documents, on computer devices or in printed form provided the opportunity to study during day trips, holidays, or any other such journeys. I found that every journey that I went on provided at least one opportunity to read documents. Of course, these travel opportunities almost never presented themselves at my optimum early morning study time, but it was a chance to learn, nonetheless. A chance that I suggest is taken, as it will maintain your study momentum. Momentum is vitally important, as well as staying on track, or knowing when to allocate more time. All of these maintain a level of focus required at higher level study within further education.

This focus does have one downside for me. It comes at bedtime. I must say that some of my greatest ideas have come to me as I am trying to get to sleep. I can't be certain, but maybe because it is the quietest and most peaceful part of the day. I am not afraid to say that at first it was annoying and frustrating, but the frequency in which it happened made me accept that my studies were constantly part of my thinking. In aid of this acceptance,

I decided to think through each idea as they came. This may be contrary to thoughts around having a notepad next to your bed to record ideas, and may not work for you, but it worked for me. For me, I slept better when I let the thoughts develop.

I cannot claim that sleeping time was my best time to focus. My optimum focus time was first thing in the morning and remains the same today. It must be understood however that given the volume of study required to complete advanced courses, any time available to study should be considered.

Develop and help others

I found during my master's study that an effective way of developing myself was to help develop others. It was rarely possible to help someone who was studying my exact subject of study, management, and leadership, so I had to diversify into other subject areas. Nevertheless, I was willing to help as I wanted others to share my passion for learning.

I did get the opportunity to assist a colleague with management and leadership a few years ago. I could not believe my luck as this colleague was studying at level 3 and really wanted to succeed. The opportunity actually came by chance. We were working together one day and had not seen each other for a few months, as we lived in various parts of England, roughly one hundred and fifty miles apart. In small talk he mentioned the that the company that we worked for had enrolled him onto the course, which was not classroom based, rather remote self-learning. This sounded difficult for him as it was clear that the company offered zero support.

Irrelevant of this, I got excited immediately by somebody else wanting to progress and offered help myself, to which I was happy that he gratefully accepted my offer. This acceptance was important as I have discovered that sometimes trying to help is lost as people do not want to hear it. To this day I do not know why such help would not be welcomed. I suggest that you accept any such assistance, especially considering that it would most probably be cost free.

During our lunch break I sat with my colleague and ran through the course brief and assessments that he needed to complete in order to pass. I spoke about needing to not just pass the course but to gain as much from the learning experience and develop his management and leadership skills. Before we knew it, lunch was finished, and we had forgotten to eat anything. I could sense that my colleague was more energised to study following our conversation.

For me this was a success, especially when I found out some months later that he had passed the course. It also came to light that many more individuals within the organisation were given the opportunity to study for the level 3 qualification, producing an extremely low pass rate, with many giving up before even submitting their first assignment. I personally believe that had support been available within the organisation, maybe in the form of mentors, then the pass rate would have been much higher. I say this as I know that it is a big ask for someone that has never studied previously to study remotely without any support, whilst also working full time. I think this approach by the organisation to educate their employees was mis-guided and destined to fail, which it did overall. A waste of time, effort, and of course, money.

My experience had taught me that developing colleagues below your own job role level is far easier than developing those above you in the organisational chart. I suppose for many people the idea of someone in lower working position teaching them something could be considered embarrassing. Of course, this goes completely against my belief. I think that we can all learn from each other. I am not in any way afraid to ask anyone for help or guidance. Remember, I have been in a position that could be considered by many to be very low on the working hierarchy, a street sweeper. I can only imagine the response by the contract managers at that time if I had even suggested that I knew something that could benefit them. I would have been laughed away.

Something similar happened slightly later in my development. I was now a service delivery manager and reporting to a very impressive and diligent manager that would go on to become a very good friend of mine, and a future business partner. This manager was different from others that I had worked with and had no issue taking advice from anyone, at any level. Always showing respect to all. This was, sadly, not replicated by his peers.

My manager asked me to support another manager with issues that he was experiencing with one of our clients. This was fine for me and presented an opportunity to show my skills, and of course what I had learned in my recent education. To be honest, I was super excited about the chance and wanted to get stuck in immediately. I did not have to wait long at all. The following Monday I was requested to attend the client headquarters with the manager that I was supporting. I wanted to make sure that I made a significant effort to help and prepared as best I could by gathering information about the issues that we were there to try and solve. It must be said that the manager I was enlisted to help did not supply me with this information. I had to search wherever I could and talk to whoever I was able to.

The meeting itself was quite frankly awful. This manager did not impress me, or the client, in any way. Some of the comments made by this manager actually made me cringe and I could not believe that someone operating at this level would think that it was acceptable. Nevertheless, I was there to help solve some issues. Issues that seemed rather clear to me. The issues would be resolved quite simply by implementing clear and understandable processes. I came to this conclusion based on another course that I was completing at this time in my development, lean six sigma. Yes, I did not have much free time as study time was plentiful with a master's degree coming to submission phase and a new lean six sigma course, but this new course I really enjoyed and would of course see it through.

During the de-brief following the meeting I presented my recommendations for solving the issues, in that processes needed to be written from scratch. I outlined my newly acquired skills in being able to do this and offered to sit down with this manager and develop the processes together, which would have been valuable learning for him that could have been used throughout his career going forward. The response he gave was abrupt and rude, which completely rejected my offer to develop his skillset. I was told plainly that this is below him and that I must go away and do it by myself. I left the meeting frustrated as I wanted to pass on my knowledge. I however kept to my word and created all of the processes required, the result of which was extremely positive.

Despite this negative experience, I will never stop offering to develop and help others, whether above or below me in the organisational chart. I have found developing others to be significantly rewarding personally and something that drives me to learn more and aim for greater achievements.

Aim higher

My most recent achievement at this time had been achieved. I had completed my master's degree. Wow. I could not have been prouder which was reflected by the congratulations and praise that I received from my family and friends, as well as university lecturers. I must say that I was completely overwhelmed by this and soaked it all up. I could not stop smiling. This was no more prevalent than at my master's degree graduation.

I had never been to a graduation before and as such had no idea what to expect. I had nothing to be concerned about. The ceremony was tremendous. I was lucky enough to have my wife, son, mother, father, mother-in-law, and father-in-law, in attendance. They were all so appreciative of this achievement as they all knew where I had started, as a street sweeping operative that had been punished for twelve months for something that I perceived to be unjust. This made the moment all the greater for me on this day. I remember thinking back to that time of my twelve-month punishment during the ceremony and in some strange way thanking it for giving me the energy to achieve what I had. Strange.

The other thing I remember from this graduation day was that my thoughts were not looking back but looking forward. As I was sat in my gown, robe and hat in my allotted seat reading the printed list of graduates, I could not stop myself from looking at which qualifications were higher than the one I was graduating for. This could have been because I wanted to continue my development, or that I was just jealous. Either way, I was thinking about the next step in my development even as I was about to pick up my master's degree certificate.

My eyes were specifically drawn towards people wearing a gown, robe and hat which were far more colourful than mine. These represented students graduating with a doctorate. Wow, what was this? It looked so very impressive, and these individuals seemed to move about with a swagger. One specific graduate walked onto the stage and took a 'selfie' with the award giver followed by a large and euphoric shout of "yes, I did it". There was a huge laugh from the audience followed by rapturous applause. This person was clearly relived to have finished the course and knew the significance of his achievement. I wanted exactly the same feeling, whatever it took.

This person graduated with a PhD. (Doctor of Philosophy), which coincidentally was the degree that I had focused on when I was reading the printed list of graduates. I don't know why I narrowed in on this, but it certainly made my decision easier, and I now knew this would be my next step. I remember being energised in that moment safe in the knowledge that my development had a newly confirmed step, even without completely knowing what was required to achieve what appeared to be a 'harry potter' level of study. If I am honest, I could not think of anything else than this even when I walked across the stage to collect my master's degree certificate.

Following the ceremony, I went for a meal with my family that were in attendance on the graduation day. Rather than having to discuss about my recent achievement, I wanted to talk about my new plan. I was aiming higher, well, this time, the highest. I had done some simple mobile phone research on the journey to the restaurant and learned that PhD. study is the highest academic level, which focused me intently. I was now asking myself whether I could reach this level. Well, why not? I had come this far without failing. Continuing my development and education was the only option for me.

I made quick progress to contact the university in aim to enrol onto the PhD. course. Things moved quickly from there. I was invited into the university to meet with the course lead which I gratefully accepted. This lady was very impressive and well spoken, using academic words that were new to my ears. I felt welcomed and for some reason comfortable in this environment. I was keen to get started, although I had to await acceptance of my application to join the course. Thankfully, I was accepted, enrolled, and set to start soon afterwards.

As always throughout my academic studies, I was in full time employment. I was used to this arrangement but not at this level of study, the highest level of education. It was in consideration of this that I decided to reach out to my employer for support. The cost of my PhD. study was high, but it was not only financial support that I was after. I wanted to be afforded some study time and to be able to discuss my studies with senior members of the organisation, mainly because I believed that my ideas would have benefitted the company.

My approach to request support was to write a formal email detailing all of the benefits to the company, which included the opportunity to focus a PhD. level study on an issue relevant in the industry specific to the organisation, something that this organisation had never experienced before. I spent weeks developing my proposal in my spare time which resulted in a professional and succinct request for support. I was really happy with it and thought that it could not be refused as I would be doing all of the work myself from which the company would benefit. I sent the email to the most senior director within the region that I operated and crossed my fingers in hope of support.

I needn't have bothered. The only positive I could take from the response was that it was fast, taking only one day in fact. It was also very brief. I cannot remember the exact wording but can clearly remember the message. The answer was no. I was used to this type of rejection from companies when I have asked if they could support me before, but this one seemed to hurt slightly more. This was because of a number of reasons. Firstly, the length of time that I was going to be committed to the study was a minimum of five years which was a huge financial investment that I would need to fund myself. Secondly, my employer showed zero interest in my development. And lastly, I knew that because of the first two points I would need to find a new career. I could no longer stay with a company that had no interest in my development. My development was so important to me, so it was time to aim higher and move on.

Elite Principe 2 – Do Something Every Day – No Matter How Small

Time to Focus – Everybody has a unique time (and conditions) that best suits their study. Find yours and maximise your results.

Develop and Help Others – Developing others will develop your own understanding of your subject area and wider subject areas.

Aim Higher – As you meet people with higher accolades than your own, know that you too can reach those heights. You have come this far already.

Chapter 8

Principle 7 - Plan Procrastination - Make It Count

Procrastinate for gain

The friendship with my previous manager progressed, so much so that we decided that we should go into business together. This was not an easy decision to make as we had minimal experience in building a viable business and it was a huge risk to us both financially should it not succeed. As you can probably guess by now, this meant for me that education was needed in this field. Our area of expertise was facilities management and our choice for a business was that of consultancy. We planned to assist others within the facilities management arena to achieve, using the skills that we had. And so the quest began to research similar businesses as well as understanding how to start a business. Quite a big ask.

The time came to make the leap into business. The company was founded, and we both moved away from full time employment. To say that I was not worried would be wrong, but the excitement of this endeavour was energising us both and kept us on track. My business partner was first to find a consultancy position. He hit the ground running and financed our first couple of months. My input came shortly afterwards with a consultancy assignment within the aerospace industry. I was ready and entered the assignment knowing that I would be successful. I knew this as I knew that I could rely on my education. The many years I had studied up to this point had put me in this privileged position and I was not going to let it pass me by.

The location of my work was far from my home, two hours' drive on a good day. This required me to regularly stay over in hotels in order to ensure that I could apply myself for the maximum amount of time without being sleep deprived and very tired. Focus was key, especially on my first assignment. Focus was, however, also required on my PhD. study. Remember, this is the highest level of study. Far more intense than anything I had studied previously.

It dawned on me quickly that in order to achieve I needed to utilise my time in the hotel. This made sense as I was in a room by myself with no distractions, and endless coffee, when it was needed. The problem was that I had no routine as I had not used this approach at any time in my studies before. The first night that I started this was actually my first night on this consultancy assignment. Funny how these things align really. I remember clearly reading the first book for my PhD. study. I managed to read four chapters only whilst making notes. Considering that I would need to read an enormous number of books and research papers for my study, reading every word of every document was obviously not possible. I needed to revert to scanning the material again and focus on the elements relevant to my study. Otherwise, I would never finish the course. I had no issue with finding this out about myself as I was evolving my study approach.

This methodology was developed further. I found that although having no distractions in the hotel room was helpful in many ways, the silence was actually rather annoying. It was difficult to study in silence. To counter this, I would have the radio on in the background, sport channels worked best for me. It was never loud, just a high enough volume that I could hear it. This did not mean that I would be fully engaged with of all of the discussion taking place on the radio. It was just background noise and I liked it. Granted, if a sport subject discussion started that interested me I would listen more intently.

I did find early on that I needed to take breaks whilst studying in this environment. My attention span was somewhere around thirty minutes, after which I would walk around the room briefly, and quite often make another cup of coffee. This was a similar study technique to the one I used in the university library, having a set walking route, but this time it was in a confined space. My hotel approach really worked for me as it allowed me to break focus in a controlled and familiar way. So much so that I developed it further.

I found that when studying in a hotel room resulted in many, many hours each session. I could sometimes arrive in the room around 5pm and have planned nothing else except to study, meaning that until I decided to sleep, I would be reading, writing, and thinking.

This was mentally draining. In addition to my brief hotel room walks, I found myself procrastinating several times throughout each study session. This resulted in me voluntarily finding other things to do rather than study, albeit only for noticeably short periods of time.

In recognition of this, I decided to incorporate procrastination into my study sessions. As for me procrastination could be building spreadsheets, reading articles not relevant to my study, or making personal fitness training plans. I wanted to make it work for me even if I was not focusing specifically on my study. So, I allotted time near the end study session to develop study plans and assess my progress and the next steps needed. Strangely, even though these actions assisted my study, they did not feel like hard work, rather like a rest from the intense focus. But it was still pushing me in the right direction. I enjoyed, and looked forward to, this time.

This was actually more beneficial than I realised at the time as it developed my computer skills which I would need to develop in order to produce my PhD. thesis. I was becoming familiar with visual progress aids by using colours to outline my achievements and directions. I find it very motivating to visualise progress and by doing this I left each study session in a positive mindset and knew exactly what I needed to do in the next study session. Interestingly, it became apparent to me that this does not need to be IT based, it can be a handwritten progress chart that is updated with highlighter pens, or anything similar. I actually used this approach if I left the hotel room to have food in the restaurant, which again ensured that my progress continued.

This may not seem relevant if you don't study in a hotel room but believe me that even if your study location is different the same principle exists. If you procrastinate it can be used for your own gain. You decide what it is you do. At this stage your studies will be a large part of what you do, and any gains are beneficial, in any form. For example, I also used to amend the signature title at the bottom of my email to include the new title that I was aiming for, Dr., during my end of study session procrastination period, of course without sending any emails with it included. This again visualised what I was trying to achieve. I did this often. It made me smile every time and motivated me greatly.

I cannot confess that this period of study was easy, quite the opposite. I was juggling being a business partner with my first ever consultancy assignment and PhD. level study, and of course family commitments. Honestly, it was a huge challenge for me. So much so that I honestly considered quitting study for the first ever time since the commencement of my personal development. Granted, this only lasted a moment, but it was a pivotal point in my aim for achieving the highest level of study.

The thought of quitting the study came to me in the car park where I was consulting during my second assignment, this time at a recycling plant in north London. It was Thursday and I had been away from my family for two straight nights, working during the day and studying in the hotel during the evening. Although this was a routine that I was used too, for a moment it seemed too much. I thought that my life could be far easier if I just focused on work and didn't have to consider study time also. The thought was real, but I saw past it.

I don't want to think of the disappointment I would feel now had I decided to quit, but that did not happen, and I am forever grateful for the decision that I made to continue. This probably only made me stronger and more focused. It is however important to know that uncertainty is not always a negative thing, well, it was not for me. It focused me even further.

Find people that listen

My experience has shown me that my developed study techniques can be replicated in different environments. Even with changing variants such as space, location, and room purpose, similar positive results can be achieved consistently. One thing I have however found cannot be replicated is discussing your studies, and associated ideas, with other people. I do not mean speaking or repeating your writing aloud as if you would when rehearsing for a stage performance, I mean intentionally discussing it with other people in order to generate debate and challenge.

For me this came in two forms, someone I knew very well and

see often, and someone that I considered competent but did not consult with regularly. They both have their benefits but are different in their availability and difficulty. Speaking with someone you know very well will be a more fluent discussion as you are used to them, and the opportunities to speak will be readily available as you see them regularly. Whereas a discussion with someone you do not see often and not know very well will be more difficult as they may not know your mannerisms very well. I will explain.

The person that I know well that I used to discuss my studies and ideas with was the person that I went into business with. There was no-one else during this period that I spoke to regarding this as I had the perfect recipient. I was extremely lucky as this person is very patient and at the same time completely honest. I felt at no point during our talks that he said something to me in these discussions simply as he thought it was what I wanted to hear. This is very important as it constantly challenged my thinking and actually made me prepare for our talks as I knew that I needed to be correct and confident in what I was saying. This was no more purposeful than when I needed to make an incredibly significant decision for my PhD. research development.

An aspect of my research was focused on lean manufacturing and utilised the acronym DOWNTIME (defects, over-processing, waiting, non-used employee talent, transportation, inventory, motion, & excessive production), the process wastes. Don't worry I will not go deep into this concept. The issue I had was that my research focus was too broad which needed to be narrowed, not an unfamiliar challenge with PhD. study I have come to understand. I was struggling alone to narrow it down at all and was in desperate need of assistance, or at least someone that will listen to my dilemma.

I remember vividly being sat in a hotel room on my own with over ten academic papers in front of me trying to reach a decision, any decision, but nothing was developing. I made the call, and as usual my business partner answered. Even though it was already at least 7pm, this person stayed on the line for at least three hours listening to my concerns, challenges, problems, thoughts, and anything else I wanted to discuss. Of course, this was not a one-way conversation. I was receiving constructive feedback throughout the conversation. After which point, I reached a decision, I would focus on excessive production. And yes, this actually did stick and formed a valuable element of my PhD. study. I may have reached such a decision without the help of my business partner, but it certainly would not have been reached as quickly, and definitely not with the confidence in which I made it during the telephone conversation. Confidence that was gained by trusting the honestly and challenge of someone I knew very well.

I know that this would not have been achieved so efficiently during conversation with someone that I did not know well. Not to say that outcomes can't be reached, but not to the magnitude, significance, and speed, that can be achieved with someone you know, and is of competence. In fact I can give an example of when a discussion with an unfamiliar person has directed my study.

I had spotted an opportunity and commenced a conversation with a well-respected expert in another aspect of my research, UK shopping centres. This person was someone that I had come to know from previous employment and was therefore slightly familiar, but in no terms a friend. I could not stop myself from talking about my study and waited for a negative response, even stopping me mid-sentence, thus finishing my attempt abruptly. Well, I was surprised. This person was more than willing to discuss my study and raised many questions about my ideas. We spoke for an hour and although it was not as fluent as the chat with my business partner, the outcome was positive. I was guided well in shopping centre classifications, a niche angle in my research question development. Success. I was certainly glad that I started the conversation and was not discouraged by fear of being shut down.

Conversely, I can provide an example of when a conversation with a person that I knew briefly led to disappointment, when I thought it would have produced a positive outcome. This was a person that held a senior position in an organisation within the industry in which our recently founded company consulted, facilities management. I reached out to this individual through an internet platform. The initial response was incredibly positive as he wanted to have the conversation sooner rather than later.

Well, that suited me perfectly as my studies were progressing at a respectable rate, without doubt in line with the timescale that I had set myself to complete. But this turned out to be a wasted effort. Once I had explained my reason for reaching out and the small talk finished his clear intention became evident. He wanted me to come and work for his company and employ my skills. What? As complimentary as this may have been, it was not the purpose of the conversation, especially considering that I had initiated it. I would like to say lesson learned, but I have truly fell for this multiple times afterwards with other individuals. I have come to understand that other people will have a different agenda than yours.

My experience is testament that you should make the effort to discuss your studies and ideas whenever possible, and with different people. But don't be surprised if they will not all lead to positive outcomes. Try anyway. As like me, it may well direct you forward whether you know the person well, or not. Do not be afraid to talk about what you do; you are 'making it count', no matter what the outcome.

Continual focus

There is no point in 'making it count' every now and then, and not maintaining your focus for the rest of your time. My best outcomes have always been achieved when my focus has been continued throughout everything that I am doing. At this point in my studies,

I used every available opportunity to learn, and even in a location and environment that you may find strange.

I was taking my son every Saturday to a martial arts and fitness gym for him to train Jiu Jitsu. The gym was open plan, exceptionally large, and would be extremely cold in the winter and very hot in the summer. This, whilst also being full of noise from people training and pushing themselves to the maximum. All conditions that were not necessarily conducive to studying you may think. Wrong. This was perfect. Well, for me anyway.

This environment was ideal for me to learn. We would always arrive early for my son's class which allowed me to occupy the one table that was suitable for me to lay out my books and papers. I got this table every week without fail. Once in position I would arrange my materials and start work during the time that all of the gym members would arrive for their classes. This was of course very loud as everyone was saying hello to each other and sharing stories prior to focusing on their exercise.

Oddly, this noise made me focus intently as I used this brief period to plan the hour ahead. Then the time came to learn when the classes commenced. This worked every week. There was not a Saturday that I did not progress academically in the gym. Bizarre words I know, but I really did progress academically in the gym environment. Which of course had the added benefit of my son exercising and learning Jiu Jitsu also. Success. I very much looked forward to Saturday's.

It was so effective that I would plan my reading around the gym as it was the perfect place for me to read. Granted it was not an ideal environment for all of my study needs. For example, it was not the best environment for data analysis or anything more technical as I was unsure how busy and loud the gym would be each week. But that actually worked in my favour as reading, and making notes, was a significant requirement of my progress and it meant that I could focus on this specifically on Saturday mornings. Which gave me dedicated time for this task and would not be distracted otherwise.

The gym environment had an additional benefit for my learning too, one that I had certainly not anticipated. I found that people in this setting were more than willing to ask questions, while at the same time be respectful of a concentrated academic reading a research paper.

Occasionally people would ask me what I was studying. Which gave me the opportunity to talk about it and further developed my understanding by having to simplify complex concepts. I simplified the concepts not because I assumed that the people would not understand, but because a full-blown academic conversation was not suitable in the gym environment. This was great for me as it made me think about my studies in easy terms and enhanced my understanding as a result.

I was utterly amazed with the interest shown in my studies by some gym members. These people were always super nice and gave me energy to continue my focus. You may be thinking that this is not a reason to join a gym, and I would absolutely agree. But this was not the case. I utilised an environment that I would have been in anyway and continued my focus to progress my studies. You can find your own environment and do the same, which will project you even further towards your goals. Make it count whenever you can.

> **Elite Principe 3 – Plan Procrastination – Make it Count**
>
> *Procrastinate for Gain – Be aware that your focus will drift from your study during study sessions. Use this downtime to progress your education by doing something fun that is still relevant to your subject area.*
>
> *Find People That Listen – Speaking with others about your study can lead to positive outcomes and at times progress your education in ways that you are unable to achieve alone.*
>
> *Continual Focus – Be prepared to study in locations that others would find unsuitable. Education at this point is very much part of your life and should be embraced at every opportunity.*

Chapter 9

Principle 8 - Consistency Over Coincidence

In the zone

Far too often are careers, and even lives, led by coincidence. The coincidence, or luck, aspect is relied on far too often and can be negated to a large degree by repeating actions that provide positive results, thus by being consistent. Although this could be considered a foundation principle as it is suitably relevant throughout your development, being consistent is no more necessary than when you want to reach your ultimate goal. Which for me was PhD. completion.

Being consistent is an easy statement to make, but takes a continued, and constant, effort. This means that even when you do not want to read a research paper, listen to a subject specific podcast, finish writing a chapter, or any other study related activity, you still do it. Not everyone will be able to do this. But at the elite principle 4 stage you are different, you know what achievement feels like and want more of it. You are focused and in the zone. And honestly, by being consistent in your approach you can predict the outcome of your efforts through observing past results.

From my experience, the alternative to consistency is achieving through coincidence. This for me has also delivered positive results but for reasons unknown and with unpredicted outcomes. But it has also produced undesired results and made me want to always employ a consistent approach. In short, if you allow your future, career or otherwise, to be guided by coincidence do not be surprised that the outcomes are not what you desire. Once you have a new direction, job, study course, or challenge, I recommend that you do the things that have previously produced positive results. Why would you choose any other way?

This was no more relevant to me than during the final stages of my PhD. This time in my study required data analysis of my research questionnaires. Although I was familiar with data analysis from my master's level study, this was a level above, a significant level above. I knew that I had to focus for a considerable length of time, which of course for me required a consistent focus. And in the approach that I found produced my positive results, I had to incorporate my study into my daily life.

In advance of starting my data analysis I had to gather my reading materials from the university. This was due to Covid-19 restricting regular campus attendance, resulting in me not being able to rely on entering the university library for extended periods of time so needed to study remotely at home. This was not a problem for me as I knew that I would be consistent in other environments too, as I proved when studying in hotels rooms in months and years previous. This time I had to utilise my house, which was actually also my place of work as I was a consultant and unable to visit clients at their offices, again due to the Covid-19 restrictions. In addition, this was also the festive period, and my son was not in school and wanted to be entertained by me, his dad. I had to juggle many responsibilities and remain focused on my study.

I set about waking up each morning at 5:30am to start my study, which was my optimum study time, as I had found out in previous years. I had lots of books to read and analysis to conduct and so as many hours that I could allocate the better. This early start allowed me a couple of hours before the working day began. It was valuable time that offered zero distractions, and as I continued this consistently it ensured that I was constantly making progress, and not neglecting my responsibilities as a father and husband over the festive period.

There was however an issue outside of my control due to covid-19. One of my PhD. supervisors (academics assigned to guide PhD. students through their research journey) was unable to return from a trip to Jordan. This was particularly problematic as this supervisor was a data analysis expert with which I needed to consult regarding my progress. I needed to find a way around this issue if I wanted to remain consistent in my approach, otherwise I would have needed to wait for him to return to England, and even possibly the university to return to normality following the covid-19 pandemic. I could not put my study on hold. I had to do something.

I contacted my supervisor in Jordan via email and hoped that I would receive a positive response. Thankfully, the response was far greater that I could have ever hoped for. It culminated in multiple online video calls to discuss my data analysis process, including meetings on both Christmas eve and boxing day. I am forever grateful for this commitment from my supervisor as it could have been easy for him to not want to work from abroad. It allowed me to progress and remain consistent.

My focus had to remain in another bizarre situation around the same festive period. I was deep in reading on afternoon when one of my sisters called to say that she wanted to visit with her boyfriend. A pleasant surprise, but I had a task ahead of me. I had to try and make the living room look welcoming, only possible by piling up all of my study materials in the corner as it was a very intense study session. Well, it needed to be as I was heavy into the data analysis.

My sister and her boyfriend had come to tell my wife and I that they were having their first baby. A monumental moment in our family. I will not lie, I found it difficult to take my mind away from the study, as it was well and truly at the forefront of my mind, but I managed to, and the result was actually progressive for me. I found that following the visit I returned to my study with a huge smile on my face. I was incredibly pleased that I was able to separate my thoughts and to return to focus immediately afterwards, I remained in the zone. A clear indication that although my study was a major part of my life, it did not damage my family relationships or stop me enjoying such memories.

And all the consistent hard work paid off, as it does. The feedback from the data analysis expert supervisor was extremely complimentary when I submitted my paper, stating "I'm proud of you". This made me feel super fulfilled, especially when I thought back to the feedback that I had in red writing from my level 7 course lead years earlier criticising my effort and application. I had certainly learned my lesson and as a result was now producing PhD. level data analysis. "Not bad for a street sweeper really", as my dad would say.

I had actually become rather fond of statistics by this point, which was quite surprising as I had not always been a fan. I recall in fact the exact moment that I was first made aware of statistics. It was during basketball practice, not where you would most expect it. We would regularly play basketball after school when I was fourteen years old as we had a new gymnasium at our school and the basketball court was brilliant.

We were joined one afternoon by one of our teachers who

actually played in a basketball league. He was very good, much better than us. But it was still enjoyable, and we set about learning as much as we could from him. He introduced us to different shooting drills, one of which was different from the rest. Our teacher positioned us an equal distance from the hoop and said, "take ten shots". I remember thinking, why ten shots? But then all was made clear. I made four shots which my teacher quickly converted into a percentage, 40%. This may seem overly simplistic, but it had never crossed my mind to use percentages in this way when I was fourteen years old. I must confess that my 40% success rate was not the best in the group, it was nearly the worst.

Following this, basketball sessions the practice had changed for me, and honestly less enjoyable. Our teacher had explained to us that our focus should now be to improve our shooting percentages. The percentages frightened me as it made me want to be better and better every time, but this was just not possible. My scoring was not improving at all, and it was really frustrating. On top of this, my success rate was now easily compared against my friends, as opposed to having a subjective view of who was the best shooter. It is no surprise that professional sports utilise statistics to improve, as it promotes competition and does not lie about performance. It may put athletes in the zone, but it honestly made basketball less enjoyable for me. Which led to me giving up.

Of course, I understand now that if I would have remained consistent, I would have improved my shooting percentages, but it really was not something that I wanted to do at the time. This zone was not for me.

Create something of your own

It became increasingly important for me to convert my academic studies and the concepts that I has learned, into my business at this point in my life, creating profit if possible. My study gave a unique insight into a specific subject, lean facilities management. I was super enthusiastic about this and wanted to develop my understanding even further, this time from a practical point of view. Up to this stage I had only ever considered it academically but was now certain that it could be used for other purposes.

I suppose I was in a fortunate position to the able to develop something unique as I was working for my own company. This allowed not only time but also resources to develop what would become the 'facilities management lean audit', an audit developed to improve efficiencies in facilities management operations. This was a very exciting time for my development as it was creating something from scratch, and there were no specific rules dictating the outcome. I could go in any direction that I wanted. It was fun, but at the same time rewarding, and also increased my understanding of my subject of study.

There is an irony related to my development of the audit and it only being possible due to my commitment to, and continued pursuit of, education. The irony being that the earning generated for my company from the selling of the audit more than covered the cost of all of my education more than five times over. Of course, my educational fees had already been paid over the years, but this is a clear indication that education can pay off in this way, if you want it to.

There was another benefit from the audit, it received a lot of attention within the facilities management arena. In addition to my company getting weekly interest from new people and companies, thus improving the database of potential customers, a well-established facilities management magazine requested to write an article about the audit. Wow, this was extremely exciting. The article was fantastic and printed very soon after it was written. I was super proud and celebrated as such with my family, and business partner.

The article was also very personal to me as it mentioned my education and how it had contributed towards the audit development. This actually generated positive communications from leaders withing the facilities management industry on an internet platform. Some of which led to additional meetings to discuss the potential utilisation of the audit.

Honestly, I had never once imagined in my life that I would create a product that other people would want, and so could be sold for financial gain. This was a far stretch from that very cold November day street sweeping all those years previous. A clear sign to you that you can achieve things that are not only far from your reach, but also of which you had never even thought of. Education opens endless opportunities.

Enjoy the outcomes

My studies had reached its concluding point. Which meant for me that I had to prepare for my Viva Voce. To explain, this is a face-to-face examination of a doctorate candidate's work, their thesis, which comes at the end of the study. The thesis being an exceptionally long essay written to present the research undertaken. I was tremendously proud of my thesis which was over eighty thousand words in total, and had taken nearly five years. However, I, like many before me, was very worried about the entire experience of the pending examination. But I knew that the end was in sight, finally.

My specific preparation began four weeks prior to the Viva Voce. Utilising many of the study skills that I had developed over the years I created countless written documents, spreadsheets, and charts, all to progress towards the big day, and keep me on track. The preparation was however not that difficult for me as I had been studying this for a very long time without a break. Therefore, I was at this point not learning anything new, rather I was refreshing my memory and preparing answers to any question that my Viva Voce panel could ask. Although I could not pre-empt every possible question.

The day arrived and I reverted to my normal strategy of starting early. Even though my meeting did not take place until 1pm, I arrived at the university campus at 6am. This ensured that I secured a large table on which I could arrange all of my preparation materials, and a large strong black coffee. I proceeded to scan my documents whilst pacing up and down the open plan reception area. I was practicing my planned answers constantly and challenging myself to remember exact statistical data. This did not go unnoticed. One of my research supervisors came to visit me. He made the comment "I have never seen such detailed preparation" which gave me immense confidence. I don't know if he intended it in the positive way that I received it, but I would like to think so. Nevertheless, it helped me.

Oddly enough, as I was walking to the meeting, I was not nervous. Not even slightly. I felt honoured to be in the position that I was and wanted to enjoy every moment. I believe the reason I had these feelings was that I was completely satisfied with my work as well as my preparation for my Viva Voce. I was justified to be there and had left no stone unturned in the entire process. Interestingly however, the feedback from one of the examiners following the meeting stated that I seemed "slightly nervous." Maybe I had read my emotions wrongly.

No matter how I read my emotions, I was successful in my Viva Voce. I was awarded my doctorate requiring only minor amendments to my work in order to graduate. I was elated. A feeling comparable to the birth of my son, Stanley, and getting married to my wife, Sarah. The relief was also enormous as the result of the meeting could have been that my work was not up to standard which would have meant that I still had a vast amount of work to complete before degree award.

I completed my minor amendments in a timely manner. Which completed my work in its entirety and resulted in successful submission. I had made it. There was now no higher level of education for me. I was now a doctor and began to use the title 'Dr.' before my name on all correspondence. I won't lie. This felt really good, and absolutely still does.

By complete coincidence, I decided now to move away from the company that I had founded with my good friend and moved into permanent employment again. Of course, with my accolades achieved through my education I gained a senior management role, still within facilities management. I joined a UK wide company as regional manager for the entire south of England, quite an achievement considering that I had only commenced my education 11 years previous.

What amazed me most by my new employer was that they were not in any way threatened by my education, as many had been previously. They embraced and it and appeared excited by what it could bring to the company. I was however fully aware that this did not make me any better or worse than my peers, but it was a clear sign that I had something incredibly unique to bring to the organisation. I had value. Or, I had developed value.

As if it wasn't clear enough that this organisation was proud of my achievement, it was cemented on my next visit to the head office. I was requested to the board room following a meeting by the managing director. I was met with a round of applause on my entrance by the directors and given a congratulations card signed by them all. It was wonderful and something I will never forget. There was one last thing, a nice bottle of champagne. If I can be a little corny, it tasted like success. I certainly enjoyed that outcome.

Another outcome of my success is satisfying but at the same time slightly frustrating. I regularly receive calls and emails offering me jobs, very high-level jobs. This is of course flattering at times; however it leaves me wondering why these people and organisations were not contacting me on my way up. Of course these may not have been high-level jobs, but companies could have taken a chance on me given my development. They did not. I am happy with that as I maintained my focus and did not think that I had reached my pinnacle too soon., which could have been easily done if I had received a job offer greater than my capability.

I remember the first call I received following receiving my doctor title. I was offered a job on the spot at twice my annual salary. No ifs or buts, twice my annual salary. Quite frankly I could not believe it and had to take a breath to let it settle in. As this was new to me, I spent the time to listen to the role and was comfortable that I would have achieved in it. But I was not interested as I was in full-time employment and very happy in my role.

Even though receiving multiple calls and emails can be annoying at times I am aware of how much of an appreciation this is of my development, and that it was this development that I had wanted throughout my educational journey. Honestly, if you would have said to me that I would become any type of management commodity when I was sweeping streets, I would have laughed at you. But I have. And I have education to thank for that. Yes, determination, commitment, desire, focus, and many other such attributes as well, but without the overall progression being driven by education it would not have happened. I am grateful for all of the outcomes that come from it.

Well, almost all of them. There was a slight issue when it came time for me to attend my graduation ceremony. I had to wait almost a year until my graduation for my PhD. due to the timing of my completion. This meant a lot of waiting in anticipation of the event. However, after twelve months the day arrived and I attended with my parents, wife, and son, all smartly dressed. This was the first doctorate in my family, and everyone seemed very proud of me. Nothing could go wrong on this day, or so I thought.

The graduation ceremony was in full swing. I was called into the line beside the stage to be greeted onto the stage for a handshake with a senior representative of the university. Step by step I was getting closer to the stage as the names were read out of the people in front of me. Now, my turn. I had a huge smile on my face and in a brief second recounted the thousands of hours I had spent studying over the years in my mind. Then I was welcomed to the stage, but not in the way I anticipated. The speaker greeted me as "Danielle". Awfully close to my name but not exactly right. Of course, I kept walking across the stage and carried out my hand shaking duty. Once I left the stage, I chuckled to myself knowing that I would forever remember that moment. I had no choice really as the short video of my stage walk that was produced for me by the university clearly shows the moment I was named "Danielle", with full audio.

Irrelevant of this, I continued my relationship with the university after completing my doctorate. This time however as a lecturer, working on behalf of the university to deliver and mark elements of their inaugural facilities management apprenticeship degree. I had now placed myself on the teaching side of the classroom as opposed to the student side that I was so very familiar with. I think I have transitioned into teaching reasonably well. I believe this to be because I knew what students want, well I knew exactly what I wanted as a student. I do not suggest that I have perfected lecturing, not by a long stretch. I am very much at the beginning of this journey. Like everything else I have encountered during my studies, I will approach this journey with consistency and determination. I will learn everything I can from it and develop even further myself. My development will never end.

> **Elite Principe 4 – Consistency Over Coincidence**
>
> *In the Zone* – *If you measure your improvement you can remain 'in the zone', a position of consistent focus.*
>
> *Create Something of Your Own* – *Your skills, developed through your education, can be used to create something that others would be willing to buy.*
>
> *Enjoy the Outcomes* – *Celebrate what you achieve and share your memories with family and friends. You have achieved. Be proud.*

Chapter 10
If I Can Do It, You Can Too

I really mean it. If I can do it, you can too. I was never given any freebies during the entirety of my studies and had to work extremely hard for an extended period of time, eleven years. But the results are amazing. I have progressed from a street sweeper to a regional manager and university lecturer with a Dr. title. This may not be your desired journey and not be the outcome that you want, but if you want a better standard of life then education has the answers. It is up to you to take the first step, and equally up to you to maintain your focus through to your desired results. Honestly, you can do this. I have.

If you choose to follow my principles and begin, or renew, your education I suggest that you should remember one important thing. The actual certificate, diploma, or any other award is nowhere near as important as the knowledge you gain along the way. It is this knowledge that will benefit you in your working life not the piece of paper with your name on it. It is very unlikely that you will be able to solve a problem by reaching into your bag and producing your certificates. It will be the knowledge that helps you solve the problems and as such will develop you. To this end, make sure that you learn everything you can from every lesson that you take.

That said, it is much easier to do this if you enjoy what you study. I do not suggest that you have to study something that you enjoy, but you do need to enjoy the study process. You will not enjoy it all of the time, especially the further you progress through your studies. At times it will be very hard, probably harder than you could ever imagine. Awake at night analysing whether you are doing the right thing may become a regular occurrence, I am sure. But these thoughts are only a sign that you are progressing as you brain will be developing too.

Expanding your knowledge is growing your own personal value to yourself and others, including any company that you work for. This will without doubt progress whatever situation you are in. Don't get me wrong, this does not result in immediate promotion on a regular basis. I am sure that you will encounter similar hurdles that I did. Employers will no doubt be wary of your development and even possibly threatened by your knowledge. But stay with it. I did and the results were astonishing. You must remember that you 'cannot grow without growing.' By this I mean that you cannot be better today than you were yesterday if you do not know more. You must constantly challenge yourself to improve. No-one will do this for you. In fact, they will be better off if you dio not improve. It would make them better.

Interestingly, some people may even want to benefit from your success. I found this out by chance. It was not until after I had completed my master's degree that a previous manager of mine had contacted me. This person informed me that a consultant that had collaborated with us many years earlier was telling the story that it was him that had developed me from a street sweeper to an operations manager. This surprised me greatly as the complete opposite was actually true. This consultant had significant decision-making capabilities when he worked with us. Considering this, I approached him for support with my development. I remember vividly how he refused to even respond to my communications. There was no support at all, but now he wanted to benefit from my success. It makes me laugh now, but it was not so funny when I received zero support.

Even without support I managed to reach my goals and much more besides. I do however regularly think back to the very cold November morning in 2010 when I was a street sweeper, and I began to daydream about what I could become. As well as being immensely proud of my achievements, I am equally proud of my journey, which includes my time as a street sweeper. I learned some useful things at this time in my life. Of these, probably the most valuable was that I could develop myself. Well, I had to if I was to rise above the manager that I thought had unfairly punished me for twelve months. In hindsight, this was a turning point in my life and gave me a solid purpose that I was motivated to follow. I should probably thank this manager for this. I certainly never thought I would ever say that but am proud that this is now my positive mindset.

Of course, this was just the beginning and the start of my journey. It is during this journey that I created the 4 foundation principles and 4 elite principles that I have explained to you in this book. Please believe me. If you set out now with the first foundation principle, find a purpose, you will be making a giant leap towards developing yourself and your education. This will start your journey and can lead to things you can right now not even imagine. It will not be easy, and will take time and significant effort, but follow the principles and you can reach your dreams.

If I can do it, you can too.

Chapter 11
Acknowledgements

To the readers. If you have picked this book up, you have the potential to reach the elite level. It is hard, but it is achievable, believe me. Start now.

My journey would not have been possible without the support of my family. My wife, Sarah, and son, Stanley, have certainly lived the entire process with me, and never once doubted me. For this I am forever grateful. Thank you so much. I love you.

My parents, Jane and Paul, parents-in-laws, Marg and Bob, my siblings, other family members, and friends, have also been supremely supportive throughout. I really do not believe that any of them can believe what I have achieved. I am truly thankful for your motivation during my educational journey and am hugely appreciative of every time you have told me how proud you are.

I also thank those that have doubted me along the journey, including those that never wanted to help me. I did it without you.

I thank my father-in-law, Bob, for giving me the idea to write this book. He made me truly understand how amazing my journey has been.

My journey would however not have started without my period of disciplinary punishment, and so I have to acknowledge the energy that the actions of my manager at that time gave me. Thank you.

Teaching wise, I must acknowledge my level 5 teacher, Sarah Stephens-Lewis at the South Gloucestershire, and Stroud College (SGS). Sarah delivered the content is an engaging way and maintained my interest throughout. Also, Slavica Talbot at the City of Bristol College, my level 7 course lead. Wow, Slavica's passion for teaching was tangible. Every lesson was unique and led to opening my mind in ways that I never thought were possible.

The university of Gloucestershire has been my part-time home for many years now and offers a learning experience that I enjoyed very much but was at the same time tremendously challenging. For this I have my PhD. supervisors, Dr. Dougie Yourston and Dr. Tamer Darwish, to thank.

My journey was however not pre-planned and as so needed some personal guidance. To name only one of many, I need to thank Derek Pettitt. Derek gave me the idea of starting an MBA and was one of only a few that believed I could do it. Thank you, boss.

I also thank, my great friend, previous business partner at Rigby Morrison FM Limited, and person that will listen to my ideas at any time of the day, Andrew Shepherd. Andrew has never doubted my ability. I wouldn't be at this stage without you, of that I have no hesitation to say. You are a fine man, an expert in your field, and have a wonderful family.

I acknowledge also Avonmouth Old Boys Rugby Football Club. I have been absent on multiple occasions from training and games with the under 13's junior team whilst writing this book. Not once have you challenged me about it. You have actually been a huge encouragement for me during the process. Thank you Tash, Sylvan, Sarah, the players, the helpers, the parents, the grandparents, the supporters, and of course the club. Your understanding is much appreciated.

This book would certainly not be complete without a book cover design. For this I have Tom O'Hagan to thank. A true professional with immense talent and creativity.

Lastly, I acknowledge further education in all of its forms. Thank you very much. I am forever grateful. I have truly enjoyed the journey so far; it has changed my life.